The Four Elements Series

Sacred Magic

A WITCH'S GUIDE TO EARTH WISDOM

Book One

Tahverlee Anglen

Sacred Magic: A Witch's Guide to Earth Wisdom—Book One
The Four Elements Series
Published by Babylon Publishing House
Buxton, NC

Copyright © 2025 by Tahverlee. All rights reserved.

No part of this book may be reproduced in any form or by any mechanical means, including information storage and retrieval systems without permission in writing from the publisher/author, except by a reviewer who may quote passages in a review.

All images, logos, quotes, and trademarks included in this book are subject to use according to trademark and copyright laws of the United States of America.

ISBN: 979-8-9920357-0-4
BODY, MIND & SPIRIT / Witchcraft

Some names and identifying details have been changed to protect the privacy of individuals.

The information in this book is for educational purposes only. It is not intended to replace the advice of a physician or medical practitioner. Please see your healthcare provider before you start any new rituals.

Cover and interior design by Victoria Wolf, wolfdesignandmarketing.com, copyright owned by Tahverlee Anglen

All rights reserved by Tahverlee and Babylon Publishing House.

BABYLON
publishing house

This book is dedicated to my muses and spirit allies, the witches of the swamp. They draw me into their depths when I need sanctuary, nourish my roots when I seek healing, and reveal the way back to myself when I feel unmoored. Every word within these pages, every teaching, is devoted to those who walked this path before me—the ones who sacrificed, so I could live this magic in my lifetime.

Contents

Part One: The Magic

Chapter One
Let the Magic Begin 1

Chapter Two
How to Use This Book 27

Chapter Three
The Element of the North 33

Chapter Four
Plant Allies of the North 51

Chapter Five
Your Body Is the North 67

Chapter Six
Winter 89

Chapter Seven
Sacred Spaces of the North 107

Chapter Eight
Dreaming in the North 125

Chapter Nine
Psychic Gifts 139

Chapter Ten
The Spirits 157

Chapter Eleven
Journeying 179

Part Two: Rituals and Spells

Chapter Twelve
How to Get Started with Rituals and Spells 193

Chapter Thirteen
Definitions 197

Chapter Fourteen
Digital Detoxing 203

Chapter Fifteen
Sacred Spaces and Altars 207

Chapter Sixteen
The Spirits 217

Chapter Seventeen
Elemental Rituals 223

Chapter Eighteen
Plant Allies 233

Chapter Nineteen
Body Rituals 243

Chapter Twenty
Winter Rituals 249

Chapter Twenty-One
Dreamtime Rituals 255

Chapter Twenty-Two
Developing Psychic Gifts 261

Chapter Twenty-Three
Additional Journeys 267

Part Three The Wheel Turns

Chapter Twenty-Four
The Final Ritual of the North 275

Chapter Twenty-Five
The Wheel Turns 279

Chapter Twenty-Six
Resources 283

Part One
The Magic

Chapter One
Let the Magic Begin

*T*HIS ISN'T A TRADITIONAL witchcraft book that will teach you which days of the week to cast a spell or on what moon cycle to make moon water. That's the easy stuff and can be found in numerous places online. This is the path of *real* magic and deep layers of transformation. Magic that you create when you look at the whole of you inside and out: the experiences, the growth, and the desires—and then *you* decide how *you* want to live. We'll explore the deep connection to the magic inside your body by spiraling through the cardinal directions, the physical elements, the spirits, and the energy that can be found around us. This journey and life as a whole are a quest for the meaning of it all. It's a journey of learning to live life to its fullest, with more joy, passion, contentment, and expression. It's the most sacred of all sacred quests, as it's a longing to discover your spiritual center and your soul's purpose. Questing for the meaning of life is a deep dive into why you were incarnated here in the first place.

You might ask what diving deep into your soul's purpose has to do with magic, let alone, sacred magic. The answer to this question is found in the elements you have already experienced in your life. When we study magic, we are studying specifically our own unique tour of years that have already transformed you and molded you into your present version. This version of you right here and right now can and will transform again; the quest is about choosing *how* you want to transform.

When we study transformation, we start with the planet we call home (the earth element) and our beliefs about where we fit into the whole (the air element), what are we here for (the fire element), and how that makes us feel (the water element). The natural elements all sit in a circular formation, and we experience them as part of the continual and beautiful cycles we call life. To study magic is to understand how these elements live both inside and outside of us and why they are connected.

A specific element corresponds to each of the four directions (North, East, South, West), and this is true in all ancient lineages and spiritual paths. Each element in each direction represents a part of you—physically, mentally, spiritually, and emotionally. When we dive into each element, one step at a time, we'll find the places inside you that have been tamed, trimmed, and molded to fit into what society deems as "good." The elements will show us where your soul is nourished and where it is starving to be set free to grow in wild and magical ways. The signs we'll use to determine what parts of you are nourished or starving will be found inside each area of your living, breathing body.

Your body is connected to the element of earth, which can be found in the North. The planet Earth itself is far wiser than us mere humans, and we can use this wisdom as a bridge to understanding ourselves deeper.

Let the Magic Begin

Your physical body is the earth, which is in the North.

Your mental beliefs are connected to the air, which is in the East.

Your spiritual passion is connected to fire, found in the South.

And your emotions can be found in water in the West.

It's all connected and it's all sacred, like one giant puzzle of existence. To complete the puzzle, you must include every life experience, every relationship, and every feeling you ever have. Each of the pieces of the puzzle are necessary to make up the complete experience of why you are here.

Picture a drawing of a circle in your mind like a compass, with the top being the North, the right being the East, the bottom the South, and the left the West. These directions are also a spiral of elements that are always in motion, and you move through them with every experience, whether painful or pleasureful, you have in your life. Now picture you—this one magical being that interacts with each of these directions and elements inside your body—yes, you, sitting in the center of the circle.

You've journeyed through elements many times in your life without realizing it. When you have gone through challenging times, you've sat in the North. Each challenge you've experienced has left an imprint on your body. When you changed as a result of those challenges, you moved around the circle to the East and redefined your beliefs. New longings grew when your beliefs changed, which is what happens in the South when you work with the element of fire. When new longings developed, new emotions emerged as you moved into the West and the element of water. Everything we experience in life can be found in the directions in the circle. Every change we've undergone can be charted as a sacred movement in the circle, and this pattern is a cycle. It's all connected and it's all sacred.

When you harness the connection between your body and the earth, then learn ancient spells and rituals, your life takes on a whole new meaning. The circle gets bigger and brighter, just as the moon does when it reaches its peak fullness. You will watch yourself open and bloom like a rose, one beautiful petal at a time, until you blossom so magically that you'll wonder why you spent so many years thinking that magic is only for magicians or only found in fantasy movies.

Spiritual blossoming, like a rose, can be accessed through the natural world that lives all around you. What's all around you is also inside of you. Each experience you've lived has imprinted you like the grooves in the bark of a tree. The imprints left on you are the foundations of the spiral path of life. The spiral path you walk in life is your own personal sacred ritual that I call magic. Sacred magic. The magic you mine for when you choose to see yourself in the completeness of the perfectly imperfect *is the quest*. Your experiences, your wisdom, the access you have to greater levels of your senses *are all holy*. Seeking sacred magic is to see that everything in your life is holy.

When we forage for sacred magic, we are taking a journey to the heartbeat of who we really are. The sacred and strong heartbeat of you longs for this adventurous trek into the unknown path and the desire for more freedom and peace that can be found only inside of you. Foraging for magic means questing for transformation that will definitely require you to question everything you've been taught to believe about yourself and the material world. When you question what you believe about yourself and the day-to-day world, you enter into realms where the nonmaterial world exists; you enter into the spiritual world.

By nonmaterial, I mean the unseen worlds, like the places of the energy of your heart, your soul, and the spiritual realm. The spiritual world is all the empty space around you. But the space isn't actually empty; it's filled with energy of all kinds: computer signals, cell phone signals, ghost and spirit signals, and plant and other nature signals. Your essence exists in the nonmaterial world, and spirits and the energetic vibration of the elements live in the nonmaterial world.

The material and nonmaterial worlds are both created entirely of energy. Learning the ways to connect to the energies of both worlds and where tangible meets intangible is where we find sacred magic in our lives.

Let the Magic Begin

Spells, rituals, and magic are powerful. But knowing how to connect deeply to the vibration of the elements is *more* powerful. What happens when you connect to the energy of the natural world (such as plants, trees, stones, rivers, lakes) and cast spells or rituals from that connection is how the nonmaterial world can be seen and felt in the material world. Everything in your daily life can become a ritual when you spiral between the material and nonmaterial worlds. Everything can become sacred when you develop the tools to spiral between the worlds of energy. Learning how to do this spiraling between the energies of these interconnected worlds is the heart of magic.

Exploring the elements one at a time in each direction and how each plays out in our lives is the key to unlocking the inner truth of your life's purpose. No amount of exploring inner truths or the connection between the worlds of energy is worth anything if we cannot use it to improve our lives. Improving our lives and seeking more freedom and joy are the point of sacred magic, because you aren't really experiencing any of those elusive and expansive feelings if you are not living at least one of your (many) life purposes. When we choose to make this a way of being and living, we begin to taste the idea of what some call "heaven on earth."

Inner truth is the wisdom of your soul and is housed inside your body. Your precious, yet slowly dying body is living, breathing, and fighting to keep you alive as long as possible with the sole purpose of feeling heaven before you die.

Your body is the vessel for your beliefs, your passions, and your emotions to be felt and expressed, and it holds it all like your personal life diary. All feelings, intentional and unintentional, live in more than just your mind. Your feelings also live inside your flesh, organs, bones, skin, hair, and cells. They're all there and can be found if you decide to take a closer look. Every emotion your body holds is connected in ways that can be found only by taking what you've known and exploring it deeper. This exploration will lead to more meaning and more truth, and will show you where magic lives, the real kind that is the result of deeply profound transformation. The kind of transformation that is so great it can only be called magic. And it is sacred.

If you choose to see, truly see, that everything is a cycle within a cycle and connected to energy both inside and outside of you, you can determine what you want to change and what you want to keep with a strong "holy yes, I love that" or a strong "no thank you." Your life, your desires, and how you want to live are up to you.

This work is already in progress and will change as you move along this path. But I will tell you that most people walk around day-to-day working and taking care of being an adult without a single clue about what their soul wants or even what it means to have a soul. I see this almost every week in my work and how impactful it is when anyone begins the process of contemplating what is housed inside their body and lets the essence of who they are be seen, really seen. When we let the essence of who we really are be seen, even just to ourselves, it can actually be felt. Wild yet real. You're doing that now just by reading this book.

I'll be your guide on this process with part storytelling and part teaching. The combination is needed to show you what is possible when we dive into sacred magic. You'll experience both the wild and painful along the way because they are both components that lead us to the experience of real magic.

To experience the magic of transformation, though, you'll first need to consider where you've assumed it's been up until now. Has it been in the material successes of the world? Have you sought after the right job or right relationship and hoped that would bring peace and magic?

I understand, as I, too, have spent many years chasing what I thought would make me happy. We've been taught to believe that striving for material gains will give us the gold star of success in life. Many times in my life I have sacrificed the development of my soul for material gains because I thought that was what I was supposed to do in order to be happy.

From the time we are young, we are taught that the way to happiness is through more money or the right car, house, relationship, or job. We've been conditioned to believe that once we reach a predetermined definition of

Let the Magic Begin

success, we'll be happy and live life the way we are meant to. In the Western world we certainly aren't taught the importance of doing meditation or breathwork, using intuition, or casting spells.

We've been told that buying the thing or having the right job title will create the sought-after feeling of life being OK and good. As if we'll earn a prize when we die that says, "#1 prize for achieving success" and a ribbon will be pinned to our cold corpse. Meanwhile, our spirit will be seeking another opportunity to come back and be a human again if not one ounce of its purpose was felt when it leaves our body.

Many people come to fear that if they don't have the things that are scripted into how we define success, they will feel less joyful and less than who they could be. This lacking leads to a continual striving for more and never being happy or peaceful with what they have. Constant striving for more and never feeling any type of joy create darkness. When darkness creeps in, it can lead you to hit cruise control and sit in this displeasure, barely getting by or worse. Living in displeasure creates dis-ease inside your body. Then judgment sets in and beliefs about what you lack can take over your body, leading to more dis-ease. Living this way is part of the cycle of life that we can choose to step out of if we so desire. We've all been there, and we've all witnessed others sitting in that place that is so far away from any type of purpose that life feels heavy, as if we are carrying a backpack full of bricks.

If there is one thing I can promise you, it's that there is a different way. Come with me on this adventure and I'll show you.

I've witnessed many people finding their way out of carrying a heavy load of bricks (darkness) by putting new rituals and new ways of moving about their daily life into place and ever so slowly, magically, removing one brick at a time until they feel lighter and freer. I've also seen the pain of continual self-judgment of never truly measuring up as a result of comparing oneself to others so often that it became a way of being. Taking the bricks out one at a time is a sacred process and is transformation of the greatest kind, self-transformation.

Self-transformation is the magic I'm speaking of. To study magic is to study transformation. When you choose the path of self-transformation, you are choosing to find a haven no matter what comes your way. You might pick up a brick for a moment or two until you remember that you can set it down again. Or maybe you will feel like you got hit with a brick and remain in a state of shock until you remember that bruises heal.

You are in the right place, even if you have not realized that happiness doesn't come from the things you have or the place you live. There is never a wrong time to work on yourself and experience the magic I'm speaking of, even if it feels elusive and it seems as if I'm speaking a different language. I will show you how in the time we spend together on this path starting in this book in the direction of the North and the element of earth.

I will teach you how to find that place inside where your soul speaks in a forgotten language that is buried underneath trauma, fear, and society's conditioning of what you are supposed to do to be happy. It's a place that can be found only when you experience the magic of life and the possibility of actually being able to take life into your own hands and mold it like a lump of clay into anything you desire. Any emotion we seek to experience, such as joy, happiness, peace, and freedom, comes from inside of us.

Here's a bold statement I want you to know, feel, and hear, right now—anything we desire to feel can come *only* from inside of us, not from any source, thing, or achievement around us. It cannot be found in another person, another job, another town; it can be found only inside us. Heaven on earth can be found in this place inside us that I call sacred magic, and it's already there waiting to be awakened.

Declaring that you can find heaven on earth inside of you is a bold claim. Yet I know it to be true firsthand from my own life and the thousands of others I've taught, witnessed, and learned from.

You will learn how to make the transition between the material world and the nonmaterial (spirit) world, where heaven and the lower levels of what you might call "darkness" can be found. The experience of the circular path will be easier when I teach you rituals to do that will soften your landing between the two worlds. I will sprinkle rituals in along the way as well as ways of working from trancelike states I call journeys.

Make no mistake, we will transition between the spirit world and the human world on this path together. In fact, I would say that knowing the large number of spirits I walk with on this path, you've likely been led right here to me and this book. I would also say it's likely that my guides and the spirits I walk with will initiate the spirits around you, too, and make themselves known, just as I was led along my own path of teachers and sovereignty creators.

Heaven on earth is what happens when you find and live from a place of knowing that everything around you, including your real day-to-day life and your physical environment, is connected. This magical and grounded way of living can be found in the sacred movement between your heart, stillness, and growth, all while living as a human and witnessing the speed of life around you. You can find this way of life mirrored in nature by looking at a tall tree that can grow all by itself on the side of the road and that stands tall amid the sweeping motion of the cars that fly by. You can choose to go to that place anytime, and as cars fly by, you can stand tall like the tree, rooted to the earth, enjoying the sun on your face. The tree does not care what type of clothes you buy or the color of your car.

The type of tree you are is based on how well you tend your soil, providing it with nutrients and water, staying tall in the storms, and spending time facing the sun. The tree that stands and grows amid chaos and takes care of its own roots is where you find your own strength to withstand stormy days. Its where you can define the real truth behind the divine desire for liberation, for the freedom to blow in the wind and for a solid foundation to feel safe.

We all carry the desire for freedom in our lives. That's what drives us to do much of what we do, like work so hard only to one day retire and be free from the weight of the expectations we think we need to fulfill in our lifetime. These expectations for many of us also stem from the need to feel safe to take care of ourselves, families, and communities.

Finding the sacred in all parts of your life does not guarantee safety from bad things happening; instead, it is the knowing that you have tools and knowledge of the bigger picture and can continue to strive for that elusive feeling of heaven along the way. That's true freedom. When you combine that freedom with the spells and rituals I am going to teach you, you'll find that even what you consider to be bad will be less and less prevalent in your life because you'll be redefining what is bad and what is good.

I didn't suddenly wake up one day and decide to pursue my soul's purpose. It wasn't a single moment that led me to shed the layers of the conditioned belief about happiness. It was a series of experiences and initiations into the unseen nonmaterial world that took me off the hamster wheel of chasing success and into the liberating sacred path of awakening.

The experiences I've lived weren't always as pretty as a blooming rose. The experiences that led me to the greatest change were the type that caused my eyes to drip tears of blood that left me drowning in sorrow. Each time I shed tears was a type of initiation into the depths of who I really am beyond this body. By initiation I mean learning the lessons of resilience and choosing to re-create myself and carry the lessons forward. Initiation creates resiliency and wisdom. Every tear of pain I have shed was an initiation to a new level of my own resilience and steadfastness.

It started with the questioning stage of a single thought that swirled for years: Is this all there is? "Is this all there is" played out in my mind with the job I had, with the way I was spending my free time, with the relationships I had or didn't have. This questioning never left my field until one day I had enough courage to actually speak it aloud. It was a choice to ask that question aloud and shift the beliefs I had carried up until that point in my life.

Everything we do is a choice. It's a choice to stay where you are, to grow, to live, to explore ... all of it is a choice. Choosing to ask a profound question about life leads to the unfolding of truth about how you've lived, what you've experienced, and what you've chosen to do with that experience. Asking these questions in search of the unfolding truths is the first step in finding sacred magic.

My own life experiences have awakened deep layers of wisdom and remembering times when I've lived before in past lives. The wisdom that awakened inside me led me to remember the fact that choice is our superpower. Choosing how I want to live led me to the path of my inner power. The inner power awakened the witch inside me. The witch awakened the spirits.

As with any self-development or self-help process, asking the question "Is this all there is?" leads to more questions, which lead to further growth, which awakens deeper levels of questions that take us far into the mysteries of life. When you step into the mysteries of life, you are again and again going into the nonmaterial world. Going into the nonmaterial world will show you there are many other energetic sources, such as spirits, allies, and forces well beyond the human realm, that you can commune with along the way.

Magic happens when we begin to explore the meaning of our own lives. When we study magic, we are studying the meaning behind transformation. The path reveals itself when we choose to see it through the lens of the elements in each of the directions. We find ourselves mirrored in nature when we stop long enough to see a zoomed-out lens of the whole picture, instead of just the small fragment we tend to focus on and keep hidden from ourselves. What we keep hidden are truths we refuse to look at, heal, and move on from.

The path of magic at its core moves around the wheel of life, starting in the North, passing through the East, South, then the West. This path of magic allows us to focus on one directional section at a time.

In the North, we explore the deep connection to the physical and spiritual properties of Earth (this planet we call home) and how our body is part of the planet's ecosystem. The North part of the cycles reveals specific types of spirits, plants that resonate with our body, feelings, and dreams. It also leads to our own deep inner wisdom, such as intuition—often called spiritual or psychic gifts.

In the East, we take what we've learned in the North about our body and our connection to the earth element, and we move it into the realm of our beliefs and thoughts, which create our life experiences. The East is the mental plane of the spiral path of magic and corresponds to the element of air. It also contains specific spirits from the unseen world, plants that help shape what we believe about ourselves, and dreams that unfold as we experience new ways of connecting with our psychic nature.

In the South, we combine the wisdom of our body's connection to life experiences, which we learned in the North, with the beliefs from the East that shape how we live, and we then express our deepest desires. The South corresponds to the element of fire, and here life moves, burns, and shakes us up. It's the feeling of sunlight on your face after a cold, rainy day urging you to dance. The South holds its own spirits, plants, and dreams that fuel our passions. By harnessing our inner fire, we awaken new levels of spiritual gifts.

In the West, all the elements and directions come together, leading us to deeper levels of emotion. The West, corresponding to the element of water, teaches us to flow. Water spirits and plants that aid in emotional understanding come to life when we spend time in this direction. We return to the beginning of the path as we see that our internal waters are the same as those of the planet. Our spiritual gifts surface through feelings and movement. In this direction, dreams are transformed, and the passions ignited in the South settle into tangible, real-life changes. Water brings the four elements into cohesion, and the entirety of who we are comes into wholeness.

It's all connected and it's all sacred.

At some point in most of our lives, we trade in freedom for more things to buy, for a busier schedule, for more of everything. When we do that, we are leaving behind the quest for the freedom we used to feel when we were five and played and romped in the moment without a care in the world.

I know what you're going to say here; you're going to say, "But I have bills to pay, responsibilities. I'm an adult now and I can't play as I did when I was a child." My response to this belief about what you are obligated to do and how you choose to spend your time is that it is 100 percent a choice you are making every single day of your life. I know hearing that you can choose, and in fact *are* choosing how you want to live your life may ruffle your feathers and cause you to wonder who I am to be telling you this. I see you in your resistance to the idea that you get to choose how you live. I see you in your resistance to the idea that you can change and do it differently, because I have been in that place of resistance too.

I will walk you through many of my own experiences of where I felt resistance to the magic of the universe. I'll share big painful truths of times I've been so buried in the underworld that I wasn't sure I would survive. By underworld, I mean the dark places we find ourselves when life gets rocky. I'll weave magic for you by taking you to places I've been that were pure, raw, and real magic. It wouldn't be the full story if I didn't share the painful parts of life that led to the greatest transformation and only focused on the wild and mystical parts of my story. This human life includes both, not just one or the other. I'll use my stories to show you what's possible. Not just this book, the North, but each book in the series will give you real life examples of what it means to travel on the greatest of quests through the spirals of each elemental direction of sacred magic. They are *big* stories of magic, tragedy, and wonder and of how deeply I've questioned my own past, present, and future over and over.

We'll move slowly in the North as we spiral through your experiences, the element of the earth, the spiritual realms available to you, and the awakened long-forgotten wisdom you've gained along the way and how it has impacted your body. It's all energy and it's all connected.

Searching for your truest, most alive self is what I call The Great Work. Exploring the elusive meaning of it all and remaining deeply rooted to each real, human moment we have along the way are magical. The magic becomes a magical *ritual* of exploration that will lead you to ask yourself what you want to feel and who your soul wants to be. Exploration and rootedness can coexist like a wild vine that grows freely in nature and wraps itself around the base of a deep-rooted tree, living divinely free to grow how it wants to grow. The vine and the tree begin to grow as one, and yet one part is solid and rooted and one can go wherever it wants. You are both the vine and the tree and can hold rootedness deeply in your body and also be wild in your dreams and desires.

You can be simultaneously connected to your human daily life and open yourself to receive messages from the spirits. Both the magical and the mystical are real and meant to be experienced as a human. As a human you are free to chase wonder and mystery and are free to root down deeper, both at the same time.

We can explore all the possibilities of real magic and why we exist *and* still handle our daily lives and the gigantic emotions we have along the way. It's not one or the other; it's both. Not doing so will add more bricks to the backpack you're carrying, and life will get heavy. Each time we stop long enough to evaluate where we are physically, mentally, spiritually, and emotionally and to take stock of why and how we got here (and course-correct if needed), we are taking the bricks out.

Finding purpose and peace and playing in the mystical realms doesn't mean we won't still experience pain, heartache, or loss; it means that the lens through which we view it all changes. When the lens of how we view life changes, it will open the ability to see what cannot be seen with our human eyes. Learning to see the unseen changes us. We can see the bigger picture and learn from it and let it move and change us along the way—like the strength of an old willow tree that over time learns how to bend in the wind but doesn't break. The willow tree has solidarity to it from growing roots so deep that it touches other tree roots and shares nourishment. The tree's branches expand out so far that they bend deeply until they curl themselves back to the earth, allowing the branches to be refuge underneath. We bend in the wind as a willow does and learn how to not break in the process; that's how life goes. Our body can root down deeply into the human world and allow our branches to expand so deeply that they curl back around to touch the earth, providing wisdom for others in the branches we grow.

In time, you'll learn that the mundane itself can be magical and your emotions are real insights into yourself. Finding magic in big, real, human experiences and letting it teach you is the same as finding magic in the quiet of winter, in a decaying forest, or in the beauty of a snowflake that falls from the sky and is caught in the palm of your hand. It's in you, and you have a quiet winter stage, a decaying of the old-you stage, and stages where you float like a free snowflake to land wherever you see fit.

There are other worlds that can be accessed as we travel this path of seeking freedom. I've spoken of some of these worlds already, such as the spiritual and nonmaterial worlds, but they are not all there is to the story of existence. They exist as places we can choose to go to or are thrust into when we are experiencing big emotions. The North is a place we enter when we are healing pain or recovering from a rupture in our lives. The ruptures or painful times are what I call the underworld, meaning you are in the depths and throes of challenging times. You go deeper into the underworld when it feels like there's no air left in your body. We find ourselves in the underworld when our passion is snuffed out and we cannot muster the energy or care to find it. We've all had times in our lives where we lose someone we love, someone betrays or harms us, or something even worse happens. If you are alive today and are reading this book, I know for certain that you have already lived through many challenges and have been in and out of the underworld too.

If we allow these experiences, even momentarily, to crush us, that's the energy of the underworld. The underworld is the only place of comfort during these times. It is not a place to be feared nor is it a place we should ever strive to remain. It exists for a reason, and I'll share examples in this book of how going into, or being in, the underworld is actually a refuge. The underworld holds comfort in our darkest times and is a place to visit when nothing else in the earth plane can begin to touch the depth of our feelings.

Because our life experiences and the big feelings that come with them remain in our body long after they have left our mind, we must allow ourselves the time to heal, release, clear, and grow. You may not even realize that your body carries physical changes from the experiences you've had in life. Experiences from profound joy and excitement to stress and anxiety all stay stuck and change how connected we are to our body, and even if we like our body.

It's big work to change the lens of how you view your body. It's spiritual-partnership work around who you were and who you are and who you want to be, and it's allowing yourself to be seen how the spirits from the unseen worlds see you. They see you as whole in all your glorious imperfections. It's soul-level work to see yourself as whole no matter how imperfect you may think you are. It's even bigger work to explore why you believe what you do about your body and to change that belief and allow your body to become the conduit between all the nonmaterial worlds.

Both viewing and changing the lens of how we connect to our body is a slow process of uncovering what lives underneath the surface of the face you show the world. It's stripping away the veil of what ancient people (our ancestors) have known for thousands of years and what we have allowed ourselves to forget: It all matters and it's all sacred. We forget because we pursue happiness through tangible things while being distracted by the shiny objects we see on social media.

Let the Magic Begin

I will show you how to see the big "c" that sits between the "b" for birth and the "d" for death. The big "c" is choice. We'll straddle the lines between day-to-day human life and the wonder of being here to experience more magic. But we must choose to change our lens and see ourselves and our purpose here, and how much bigger it is.

The unseen becomes visible when we choose to see it. Using this book we will start at the beginning of the cycle itself and look for deeper meaning to find more of what feels like heaven on earth and less that feels like chasing an empty dream. The physical, mental, spiritual, and emotional aspects of yourself can, and will, change as your life progresses. The big "c" is choosing to make meaning of it all, giving each experience purpose.

Once you realize it's all connected—every experience, every person, every single magical synchronicity that seems random—then you learn to not hold on too long to what happened yesterday or the day before. When you realize it's all connected and what happened yesterday impacts today, you also know what you do today will impact tomorrow.

Combining the understanding that it's all connected and that we are always choosing with what we *want* to experience, and making changes based on these concepts is magic in its raw form. And this combination of how everything is connected and we are always creating and choosing is the baseline we'll use to cast spells and use rituals to move our life into the direction we want.

We start in the North, sitting in the top quadrant of the circle of life, to activate the magical connection between the cyclical nature of our body and the element of earth. Sitting in the North is merely a stop along the path to finding yourself, yet it is fundamental if you truly seek to find the most whole version of your body, mind, and spirit. If exploring magic means exploring transformation, then we start with you, your body, and your connection to the element of earth.

While sitting in the North, I will lead you through the most important aspects of this direction in Part One.

- The element of earth itself and its energetic imprint.
- How working with plants and trees are your allies in magic.
- Why it connects to your body itself.
- How the North impacts the winter of your soul.
- Why your physical space and dwellings influence your vibes.
- How dreaming can aid you in seeking answers to your greatest questions.
- What psychic gifts we all have access to and how to use them.
- Introduce the spirits that live in the nonmaterial world that want to work with you.
- How to journey into the spiritual plane to be in community with them.

In Part Two, I'll provide specific rituals and spells to support the entire expansion of your being while in the North.

We'll sit a while here, in the North and take refuge among the trees to explore our own roots (our body) and smell the sweet and enchanting life that lives inside a single flower bloom (our connection to earth). We'll travel into the swampy, murky waters of fear in a quest to awaken dormant knowledge (what stops us). We'll find our own shine in each experience we've lived and explore if we've allowed it to teach us (expansion) or diminish us. My life story and the stories I share about clients and students I've worked with will show you the real-life magic of transformation and that it's real. It's not a fairy tale I'm sharing; it's a real declaration that there is another way to do this thing called life, and it's magical as fuck.

This is my life's work, taking you on the quest for the freedom you crave that lives in the center of your belly. Everything is a cycle, and we start to see the meaning of the cycles of our lives and let nature teach us how to work with not against the cycles. We'll find the connection in the cycles of nature and life, then we'll utilize that connection to awaken our own knowledge and wisdom along the way.

Let the Magic Begin

Let me tell a little about myself and how I do this work.

My life, over time, has become a quest for liberation and reclamation of glorious joy that I live and teach, called real magic. I am a witch and woman, and I cast spells that create every aspect of my life. My life is a continuous journey of letting go in order to see new connections and magic in what's to come while being firmly planted in today. I commune with spirits and use my psychic gifts to teach me what my human life means and how to make the most of my time here. I spend time in nature every day as a way to explore the journey of the cycles I am living and the teachings I create.

As a warrior for truth, I carry potent medicine that heals your heart and releases you from what weighs you down and keeps you from the sweetness of freedom. It's a gift I'm proud to call my own. I am a High Priestess who carries the sword of initiator in the school I founded called the Moon Temple Mystery School, where I help thousands of souls define their own version of magic—the real kind that is measurable in how much happier and fulfilling life can be.

I am a channel to the underworld that shines light on the shadows of darkness where pain lives. I am wild at heart and like to move among the spirits of the dead to deliver them flowers and remind them they are not forgotten. I am abstract and I celebrate the beauty in my abstractedness. I see you in your abstractedness too; it's a beautiful sight to behold.

I've initiated in many organized traditions such as the Sacred Way, as a High Priestess (based in a closed practice similar to the Golden Dawn), and in the Celtic Mysteries, and have received the Eleusinian Rites. I've worked with mentors who are shamans, oracles, Druids, mediums, death doulas, ministers, tantras, witches, and countless other wisdom keepers who have, and continue to, guide me on my own path.

In every instance I learn more about myself and how I am not the honey that the bees make; I am the nectar they pick up and carry plant to plant to keep the flowers blooming. I am not the cosmic and beautiful rainbow you see in the sky after a raging storm; I am the rage that fuels the storm.

My soul and my spirit speak loudly at this stage in my life and are constantly reminding me of one of my life's purposes, which is to be, see, and honor the rage that is so often repressed in others. It is a rage born of not seeing the power and beauty that live inside us and that have been trampled down through living human life. I rage for your own self-repression. I rage for beings that feel like they are put in cages and do not know that they hold the key to be set free. I hold and transmute rage for every bit of unhealed trauma that stops you from being deeply connected to your body. I allow rage to fuel me to enter the underworld alongside you as many times as it takes until you find your way out. I rage for the humans who have died for using magic and talking to spirits.

I am not the moon goddess that charges her crystals under the full moon; I am the witch queen who anoints her third eye with blood and gets down on all fours under the moon and prowls alongside the spirits of witches that have come before. Those spirits of the witches that came before us also see you in your full glory. It is an act of pleasure and service to celebrate the spirits that dwell among humans to support the awakening of the true nature of what they came here to be and experience.

I carry the scars of this lifetime deeply hidden under my skin, and I honor them often with blessings of gratitude because I know these scars make up all the parts of who I am today. I will teach you how to view your scars as the sacred creation of who you are today too. This vulnerable part of me that holds these secrets close inside has been cracked open in this book for you to see that you are not alone in the scars you carry. I know you have them. I can feel them.

I carry oracle codes like a road map to the cosmos in ink on my flesh. I wear a cloak that has boundless pockets of magical tools always at my disposal that I can cast at a moment's notice. I nourish the power of my heart in all things and can teach you to do the same.

I am here for this moment, but I know I cannot stay. I cannot stay because, most of all, I am a student of life, and with every new facet of knowledge I gain, I change.

Let the Magic Begin

You will also change with each facet of knowledge you gain. You do not need to embrace the label of witch to do this work; it's for everyone who desires to shed the layers of their old selves in order to be their best selves.

Now that I have let you into self-defining truths, let's talk about the word that you've read several times so far that likely gave you a little wobble of discomfort. Does the word "witch" unsettle you? Or maybe it was the visual of anointing my third eye with blood? Both of these are real and true: I am a witch and I often anoint my third eye and others' third eye with blood. I use blood in rituals and ceremonies because it signifies our greatest power—our power to live in this human body. Blood represents life force energy. Blood represents the unseen life force that most of us don't even think about unless we are injured or our skin is cut. Yet it flows continuously through every single part of our body. Blood is why we are here and alive.

I define "witch" as one who has access to knowledge and chooses to live life on their terms, honoring the connectedness to it all. Making the connection between the elements and cycles is witch work. Defining truth and how life changes and moves is witch work. Seeking more, questioning deeper, and listening are the foundation of how all successful and powerful spells work.

If you quiver a little when hearing the word "witch," it's because you have been conditioned to believe that it means dark and scary, and there is truth in that in the same way as with great power comes great responsibility. You need only to turn on the news for five minutes to realize dark and scary are everywhere. The word "witch" makes many people uncomfortable, as they feel fear from thousands of years of being told that power shouldn't be ours—it is only for the holy that lives outside of us. You fear it because the word has such a significant charge to it from years of (mainly) women being persecuted for anything that can be classified as witch work. We all carry this in our bones from our ancestors, from our conditioned beliefs, and from the belief that having your own personal power to create change for ourselves is bad and evil.

Sacred Magic

This series of books will challenge you to redefine what all words mean to you, not just the word "witch." I will challenge you to redefine every aspect of your beliefs about what's real and what's fantasy (such as the beliefs you hold about yourself that were programmed inside you from others). We'll explore where you were the victim of circumstance or if you made choices that led to a lesson to be learned. When you learn to take responsibility for your choices, you learn self-awareness, which leads to understanding your greatest power lies in your ability to choose. It's all connected and it's all sacred.

Here's the thing: Choice is powerful because when we realize we are constantly choosing, it means we can choose something different at any point and time. When we choose something different, we can actually change. Choosing how we want to live is the heart of this work.

I identify with the word "witch," as a way of reclaiming my ability to choose every single aspect of my life. I wear this ownership like a warm, comforting blanket of responsibility to myself first and to the world at large. Living the witch life as the way of choosing the lens through which I view life and create from is plain and simple. I can choose how I want to live, how I want to heal, how I want to teach, how I want to be on an endless passionate pursuit of experiencing joy. I can choose to create a positive impact on the world. Choosing the path of service to myself and others is all witch work to me.

I cast spells in my pursuits that are a type of prayer. I host rituals that start with learning how to expand your energy through your breath and by connecting your body to nature before setting powerful intentions. And yes, I cast spells that include raw power such as blood as a way of expanding what I know is possible with raw power. Although I will not talk about blood rituals in this book, I will lead you to your body as the starting place to understand why blood (and our body) is the vessel of such power.

You can take a deep breath now knowing there will be no sacrifices in this book or any type of rituals that you might deem as dark. Instead, in the North, we'll focus on connecting to nature as a new way of being when you begin to choose how you want to live.

No spell can overcome a belief you hold onto tightly. When you hold a belief so tightly, it's like wrapping yourself in barbed wire and nothing can get near you, nor can you move. Removing the barbed wire can be done in several ways, one being to actually let your flesh bleed and feel where the binding exists; we will not do this in this book, but it is an option that I have leaned on many times for those who need it. Or we can start by understanding why your beliefs are wound this tightly around you so no new growth can take place. This is the sacred part of magic, the initial steps of exploring how we got here before we dive into advanced layers or spells and rituals.

Beliefs are not facts; they're thoughts or experiences you've had over and over again to the point that you believe them. Regardless of if a belief is factual, if you believe it to be so, it will become your reality.

Beliefs like barbed wire not only cut anything around you, but they also cut YOU, deeply.

I will not battle you to remove the barbed wire that binds you to your old story or old ways of being. What I will do instead is show you that you need only to remove the wire and begin unwrapping it from the painful place you've carried it. The wounds of the wire against your skin will heal and fresh skin will grow. New skin will hold possibility and joy. Releasing the binding will open your life and your connection to your purpose in wild and wonderful ways.

Witch work at its core is the choice to see how everything is connected and the choice to see it all as sacred. Working the spiral path of magic is then taking that lens of everything being sacred and exploring what you truly want to live and experience and intentionally making it happen. Witch work is also a deep remembering of the wisdom that lives in your body that craves to be awakened. It's the call that leads to the question we ask in the first place, "Is this all there is?"

It makes no difference to me what label or word you use to describe yourself; you are many things all at the same time. The work we are doing on this path of sacred magic is a mystical voyage to the real you and it is for everyone. I'm not here to convert you to witchery or take away from what you believe about the source of the divine or God; it's all welcome here.

What I will do on this journey is show you the way to begin unraveling where you feel you are not in control of your life and how to take control back. I'm here to help you find your own sovereignty. While we are in the North, we will explore in depth what is waiting to be discovered inside you.

- The element of earth and how it is mirrored in your flesh and bone.
- Plants from the bounty of earth that can heal you and change you, and where to find the medicine of your spirit in all things that grow.
- The importance of connecting to your physical body and how it holds the keys to your own magic.
- Why sitting in the North is connected to the feeling of being in the winter season and how to allow yourself time to be in the winter anytime of year.
- How to use the energy of the North to create sacred spaces in your home and how doing so will change every aspect of your life.
- How your dreams change and flex in all directions and using that to impact your dream state.
- How your body receives knowledge from the spiritual realm, which are your psychic gifts.
- How to lower the veil between you and the spirits that exist in the direction of the North to gain wisdom and knowledge from those no longer living.
- How to alter your mind and go into trance states to move between lifetimes and spiritual planes to see the unseen.

Let the Magic Begin

In Part Two of this book we will go even deeper when I teach you rituals you can do to anchor yourself into an embodied way of living for each area we uncover.

To go on this magical adventure together, I must ask that you be willing to be undefined for the moment. We will take the spiral path together, one step at a time, starting here in the North. When you are ready to move out of the North, I will lead you in the next books through the East, South, West, and then back to the center, where you will find yourself. This journey is the path of sacred magic.

And so it will be.

Chapter Two
How to Use This Book

SACRED MAGIC IS A QUEST to find your soul's purpose and understand how real magic works. Real magic is about transformation. Questing is about finding truth and purpose with a set outcome. This book is for you to understand how questing for your soul's purpose and allowing yourself to be undefined for a small slice of time mean setting down the backpack of bricks for a little while. It's time, dear friends, to take a few deep breaths and enjoy time with a tree instead.

Read this book and know that you hold possibilities in your hand more powerful than anything you can buy. You are holding possibility in your hands that speaks of freedom. This book will be a magical map to connect to the spirit world and bring allies forward that live in the nonmaterial world. I'll share my magical map and the map I have created for others as glimpses of where magic exists.

Begin a journal and title it with your name and start taking notes about yourself in the North. I have a journal specifically to help you with this that you can use as a companion (see all supportive documents and books at Tahverlee.com).

Here are the steps to make the most of this book:

1. Read all the way through once, making notes along the way of anything you've learned or questions that arise inside you. You can mark the pages with a pen or fold down the corners you want to return to.
2. Read each chapter one at a time and at the end of each chapter, go to Part Two and find the rituals to practice. Choose one or two to begin with.
3. Use the contemplation questions in each chapter as ways to reflect back to yourself where you are during this time of your life. Journal often on how you feel visiting the North. Some questions will resonate deeply and some not so much; it's all welcome. Be aware that the questions you brush off as not for you are often the ones that will provide the most clarity: Start by writing out the question and why you think it's not for you.

In order to get the most out of your time in the North, let's consecrate this book, in any form you have it, as yours.

How to Use This Book

Consecration Ritual

To consecrate an item, such as this book, is to intentionally choose to make it sacred. Consecration means to turn the ordinary into a vessel for transformation. You can add external energy to the book by claiming it as your own. It's a powerful way to lock in your own power and honor the sacredness of your path of magic.

Steps for consecration of the printed version

1. Write your name on the front and back covers. Under your name on the front cover, add something you know to be true about yourself. Start with an "I am ..." statement such as a mom, a student of life, a seeker of knowledge, a lover, a daughter, a son, an author, a witch, a child of god, or whatever feels right. This will be your first of many "I am" statements you will learn as you continue on this journey. Start with what feels true in this moment. If you don't know what to write about yourself, start with two words: "I AM."

2. Find something from nature—a leaf, a flower petal, a small branch, a sliver of a stone—and add it to one of the pages in the back. This is to represent the direction of North. Think of adding something of the earth to the book that can be flattened between the pages. A rock, for example, is better added to your altar as it would fall out of the pages if you tucked it into this book.

3. Even though this book is focusing only on the elements of earth to the North, in order to do a full consecration, we need to use all of the elements. For the East (air), add an item such as a feather, a drawing of a feather, or a wand, and pass it through a smoke blend or give it your breath. Speak your name into the opening of the book where you've written your name to infuse it with your own magical air. Ask the book to show you what is for you to take away and breathe heavy

onto the pages to awaken what is for you with the power of your breath (air magic).
4. To add the element of fire, you can draw what fire feels and looks like to you anywhere in the book or on the cover. You can hold it over a flame (but not so close that it catches fire) or even add a picture or item you are passionate about inside the pages.
5. Add the element of water to the book with a droplet on the front and back covers. The droplet of water you add can be water from nature such as a lake, ocean, river, or pond. If an outdoor source of water is not handy to bring the element in, try morning dew, snow, or a droplet of rain. You can also add water by letting your hands drip onto it after a shower or bath or even drip a bead of sweat.

When all four elements have been added and you've claimed the book as yours, the ritual is complete.

Steps for consecration of the audio version

If you are listening to this book with the audio version, start a journal and do the same steps above but use your own personal journal.

Optional items: Use paper clips, markers, pencils, or anything else you desire to add and track items in the book. I give you full permission to create magic with this book and if that means writing over my words, drawing, painting, stapling or attaching, then go for it. I will celebrate combining my words and magic with yours while we spend this journey in the North together.

As you read this book and remain undefined for a moment in time, enjoy the moments with yourself. Being in the North on this journey means feeling deeply into how you define yourself. You are at a place of remembering who you are and who you want to be. Being undefined means clearing your field, energy, and beliefs to allow the nonmaterial worlds to swirl into the material worlds. While you are on this journey in the North, I will hold the vision of

How to Use This Book

your own liberation close to my heart. I will hold you in your liberated version. Take a break, even momentarily, from the sparkle of quick dopamine hits from the human world that comes in the form of social media likes, new shiny toys, and most of all, others' opinions of you.

The North is where we begin.

Let's go.

Chapter Three
The Element of the North

THE ELEMENT OF THE NORTH is the element of earth and the planet we call home. The planet Earth is not only where we live, but it is also a place we are deeply connected to, as our energy is interwoven with the natural world. The natural world is everything that is alive, such as plants, trees, animals, all bodies of water, and the energy that moves among them. We are one component of the energy that creates the whole of this place we are bound to by the law of gravity.

There have been many times in my life that the earth has been the place I go to shed pain. This great planet we live on has medicine in the form of natural energy that lives in all things. Even if it's the winter and nature is taking a rest, its energy can be felt and utilized as an extension of ourselves. Getting outdoors and going for a walk without any devices or headphones will awaken your senses and let you explore the part of nature that is awake and talking to you.

It's funny to me that the youth today call going out without a device or headphones "going naked." We've gotten so far away from being with ourselves that we feel naked by walking or going out without a device. Our need for constant distraction from our true feelings and thoughts is poisoning our body, mind, and spirit.

You can go to nature when you can no longer hold big emotions that live inside you, but you will need to do so "naked."

I'm going to tell you about one of those times.

It happened one day years ago when I was writing my memoir. I booked a stay in the mountains of the majestic and awe-inspiring Rockies in Colorado during the writing process. It was the start of the COVID-19 pandemic, and both my grown babies were at home plus many of their friends. It was a time of many late-night parties in our pajamas with cookies and games. It was blissful considering what was happening on our planet. Shutdowns, masks, and a complete stop to life as we knew it.

While this was happening, I was in the deep throes of capturing the most painful and transformative moments in my life. I was working with a writing mentor who was helping me find the threads of what made me the magical human I am today. A large part of that process was to write the real, raw truth, not the sunshine and rainbow version. Which meant that I was time weaving, ritual crafting, and capturing the sacred cycles of death and rebirth that I have lived through many times in my life. I was writing about trauma and pain, much of which I had never discussed in detail with my children. I craved solitude and to be shrouded in the fog of the cool mornings in nature, alone with my pain. I wanted the deep darkness at night to sit by the fire with my heart cracked open to write and allow myself to feel it all. I had a good friend who owned a cabin that I decided to rent for a week at a time. I spent time at home for a few weeks living normal life, or at least what the new normal was, then I retreated to the mountains where I bled onto a page.

One particular week of writing, I was hurting from remembering a painful time when my then-husband (and father of my children) had an affair with one of my best friends. I was reliving the memory over and over to capture it for my memoir.

I was reliving that time and reliving the emotion and shock. Although it was many, many years ago that the affair happened, and I have healed from the trauma of losing my husband and my friend, it became a return to a painful time I had left in my past. Each word I typed and each memory that came was a descent into the places I didn't want to be.

You know these moments, the ones in our lives that just thinking about can turn our stomach into knots so tight that we feel like we could die from the pain? This was one of those moments.

It was so far behind me, and years of therapy and growth had all but erased this time from my body, but this time-weaving moment of magic made it seem real and fresh all over again. I had completely forgotten certain details of that treacherous and life-altering time, such as the fact that I had found them in a car together and had walked up and punched him straight in the face. I was equally fascinated and appalled to recall the way my body and mind reacted in those moments in the weeks and months following the discovery and how real it felt again in the reliving of the experience as I wrote it down from a place of truth.

It's like I was right back in that time where I had disconnected from my body. I wasn't calm and sunny as you may know me to be now. I was that storm of rage that wanted to burn down many people's lives, including my own. I felt like a feral cat, wanting to bite and scratch and make others bleed. Because I was bleeding inside my heart. This was a return to the underworld.

The emotions were so big that the walls of the cabin felt like they were weeping with me. The air outside became still. The clouds overtook the sun as if I had brought on the darkness.

And then I felt it. The feeling of death. Death of relationships. Death of ideals and morals. The rancid smell of burning of relationships, the pain I had felt so deeply from that time that caused me to lose one third of my body weight. The shame discolored my skin to a pale color. I knew on a conscious level that I hadn't died from these endings, as I was here writing about it almost twenty years later, but here it was, the feeling of death all around me. It was my own death I was remembering. A part of me had died during that time.

I was alone in a cabin far away from any town or friends. Far away from magical tools and altars. My phone was off, and I was truly alone with myself. The goal was to write the story, and the result was a reactivation inside my body.

I didn't forget, not for a single moment, that this experience was one of the anchoring experiences that led me to who I am today. I knew it. I felt it. And I was ready to finish the writing and put this decaying old death back to bed, deep in the center of the record of my soul as a stepping stone to who I was today.

But my body had not yet released what I had called forth. It was time for the witch work that I had brought into my life since then. It was time to call in the magic needed to transmute this dark, heavy energy that I brought into the current moment and to step back out of the underworld.

I needed deep levels of magic and a ceremony to honor the part of me that I had weaved back into the here and now from the revisiting of this time. A ceremony to let my body bleed it out again and find my way back to my center. The place I had fought long and hard to get to since this had occurred.

I needed to go to the earth for re-healing.

Even though I didn't have my magical tools or altar space (only one small cauldron for incense), I knew I had access to all the elements in nature itself, and I began planning a ritual to honor the time when the pain was so great that I thought I would die.

I planned the ritual that would take place at sundown while I was still at the cabin, beginning outdoors and finishing in the bath. It took momentous effort to plan and create the healing ritual, as I was lethargic. My body felt heavy and laden down from this revisiting of that version of me.

The ritual was:

Earth: Go directly outdoors in bare feet to give this pain to the earth to be transmuted.

Air: Speak and chant alongside sacred smoke to release unspoken, over-spoken, and old wounds that had resurfaced.

Fire: Stoke the fire and sit by candlelight to celebrate how I grew from the ashes of who I once was.

Water: Ritually cleanse to allow myself safe passage back into my body.

I lit the candles. Stoked the fire. Hummed and chanted to myself while preparing, as if I were comforting that young woman who had in one fell swoop lost so much. I closed down my computer and put away my writing tools. I brewed a fresh tea of mugwort and lavender and let my tears fall into the pot.

Then I allowed myself to sit with it. No writing. No time weaving, just allowed myself to feel what my body was feeling. It was grief that I was feeling. The grief came roaring back from the friend I had loved and trusted with my most intimate secrets who had chosen to have an affair with my beloved husband. Raging grief for the man I had married and whose babies I had carried in my body and birthed into the world. A man I loved deeper than any other human to that point in my life. And fuck, the remembering hurt so bad again that I wanted to throw up.

I allowed myself to grieve again, no matter how long it took. I swayed, rocked, moved, and ached. My eyes leaked holy water for hours, still chanting, and at times falling down onto my knees and heaving with anger and pain.

And then there was a pause in the way my body was expressing. Once that pause came, I knew it was time for the ritual. I went into the bathroom and ran a hot bath for the last part of the ritual. I burned large pieces of copal on my incense burner, the only magical tool I had brought with me, filling the cabin with smoke.

As the sun began to set, everything was ready, and I opened the back sliding door and walked down the stairs to the barren and cold winter earth in my bare feet. I stood at the edge of the cabin with miles of mountains and fields around me and let myself just feel it all. The pain, the hurt, the vulnerable feeling of loss. I began to cry again with guttural sounds.

With each new wave of pain, I cried louder, letting my voice be ravaging. I took a step farther away from the cabin and farther along the earth.

I could feel the places in my body where the pain lived, and I bent down and gave it to the earth.

I cried, I walked, I moaned, I screamed, and I eventually fell to my knees on the earth and rested my head on the dirt, too tired and too raw to move. I sat there with my forehead touching the earth and my body resting on my bent knees for a long time. It was now dark, with only the stars to be seen. The tears slowed down until there was only a trickle left.

I began chanting and releasing—*please take this heaviness from me again and show me the way back to my center.*

Over and over I chanted, and my breath began to slow, and the tears stopped. The moisture from the holy water coming from my eyes had created a little puddle, and I could feel the cold, wet dirt under my forehead. I felt weak and exhausted, but the heaviness was gone. I was able to get up and begin making my way back to the cabin.

I crawled into the warm bath to ease the transition back to my center. I sank deeply into the warm water with only the flames from the candles as light. I could hear the fire crackling in the other room, and my body slowly returned to the older, wiser version of itself again. I felt this painful time from twenty years ago begin to fade into the past where it belonged.

Then I closed my eyes, and it was as if I were looking at myself from above. It was me, a flesh and bone body, but it wasn't me; I was a rainbow of light. Then a body again. Back and forth the vision of myself swirled. My human body was full of emotional scars that had appeared like recently healed cuts from a knife all over my skin. The scars were pulsing light. Both one and the same, I was seeing myself float in the water. Ever so slowly, each one of the scars that had once lived in me began to pulse. With each pulse, a vine began to grow from each scar. I was witnessing my own body begin to grow vines. The scars were the seeds.

The earth and I became one, and my scars changed into ripe, fertile ground for new growth, just like when you trim a plant for new growth. The place where you cut looks like a raw, open part of the plant, but it becomes where new growth can begin. The scars were the foundation of who I've become since that time.

I know how much I have grown in resilience and strength after that section of book writing. Nature is a powerhouse of transmutation when we ask it to be. This planet, our Earth, has no limit on how much emotion it can feel from its humans. Earth is our great mother and her vastness can hold our bigness. This is the power we have available to us anytime we connect it to the earth. You just need to step outside and put your body on the earth to feel her.

That's what I did when I needed to bury the part of me I had called forth while writing my memoir. I went to the earth first. I gave my pain to the barren and cold earth so I no longer had to hold it. She, the great mother, held me while I wept and grieved.

I didn't have the tools then that I do now to process all of what was happening in my life. Looking at it from today's perspective of my soul's yearnings to be here, right now, doing this work alongside you, it's clear to me that the relationship I had then wasn't the relationship that could hold me in this stage of my life. Instead, it was the relationship that resulted in the creation of the two greatest loves of my life, my children. And more recently, my grandchildren.

It was, and still is, all connected. The lessons are connected, the resilience is connected, and the depths of pain and love are all connected. It's all connected and it's all sacred.

When we feel joy, we can give it to the earth, and she'll celebrate with us and feel our emotion. When we feel pain, she'll hold us, and the energy will help restore our feelings. Any and all emotions can be balanced and held by the earth. This is why we call her the great mama—her arms and capacity are endless.

Exploring the North means exploring how to connect to places in nature to find refuge and knowledge and awaken forgotten wisdom. In elemental magic, the earth is often associated with crystals, plants, and blooms. That's the surface, the low-hanging fruit that can be easily reached and built into our daily practices. But there's more. There is a vast awareness of what we can access when we look at spiritual and physical properties that live in nature.

We are vast in our emotions and how we process them. We have the largest range of possible feelings accessible to us within our body, and each of those feelings can be found and explored in the natural world. The natural world is us and we are it.

Watch a plant that grows indoors or outdoors and you'll see your own cycles in the plant. It will need water and sunlight to survive, as we do. The plant will shed its old leaves to make space for new growth, exactly how we do when we change and grow; we also shed old layers to make space for new growth. The plant will have seasons of growth and bloom and seasons when it's quiet and resting. It needs nourishment from the soil to grow strong roots, just as our body does. And we both (and all living things) require water to survive. All the elements we need to survive and thrive are sacred.

Branches of trees break and bend in storms and can appear devastated but have roots that continue to live and grow. We can break and bend in the storms of life and can feel crushed by the weight of that and still continue to live and grow. When I felt like I was completely decimated by my pain, my roots, too, were alive and learned how to regrow. When trees are rooted down deeply into the earth, their branches can reach higher and higher to the sun.

We go to nature because it holds the medicine our body craves. The real medicine that has been accessible to us for thousands of years that we've forgotten. It's right there in both physical and spiritual form whenever we need it. And we do need it often. You need to spend only ten minutes on a stressful day going for a walk to know this is true. You can gently bring a fragrant flower to your nose and inhale its beauty to feel an immediate uplift in that moment. Or put your hand on a tree. Or lie in a field of grass. You can at any time, stop and feel the energy of earth if you pause long enough to do so.

This is witch work, and the results are sacred magic. This is what we do when we are in the North and learning about the element of earth. We first learn that it can be felt inside of us when we spend time in nature. A gigantic rupture in your life is not necessary for you to need the North and the medicine the earth holds. It's something we need during all the moments in our lives—big, small, painful, joyful moments—all of it.

We've lost this connection from years of looking at a device in front of our faces instead of staring at a tree and listening to the birds that inhabit it. We've traded putting our feet in the grass for a social media post that has a picture of the grass.

Finding what is sacred inside you means taking a moment here in the North to sit with yourself as if you are a great willow tree and look at how your branches have bent and contorted, and consider why.

I've often said in classes that I teach in mystery school, that our body used to be a cell phone. That we felt the signals of our own heart rate and our own energy, and that of others. We detected the changing seasons by how nature felt. We predicted storms by listening to the wildlife outdoors. It's all still there if we can be quiet long enough and listen. We didn't rely on a device; we relied on our body, and that is because of the intricate nature of how our body is connected to everything that takes place on this planet. It's all energy. Elemental energy.

I know you will not doubt that everything growing outside in nature is alive. We know this. To do the work of finding and crafting your own powerful inner haven means to listen to all living things, not just those that look like you. We are of this planet. We are made of this planet, born of it, and will return to it.

There is a place on our planet for technology and growth, and yet there is also an ancient place we can awaken so we can remember how to connect to our own deepest wisdom centers that live within our body and are part of this intricate web that lives on this planet. Technology cannot replace the feeling of lying down and resting under a tree or walking out your front door after a rainstorm and smelling the fresh earth combined with rain.

There are entire universes in a single leaf of a tree. There are entire universes in a cell in our body. The roots of a tree grow deeply down into the earth and into the soil to reach nutrients and sustenance to be able to survive and grow. There are roots within our body, our spirit, and our soul that also desire to root down and connect to sustenance in order to fulfill our purpose.

We can study anything around us in nature, no matter where we live or what the climate, in order to reflect back to ourselves where we may or may not be out of balance within ourselves. Whether we're searching for health or the spiritual, the mystical, the magical, or even for meaning, it can be found by studying these exact same principles in a small square patch of nature around where we reside.

Earth can also be the medicine we need when we face big life changes, both the traumatic and the exuberant.

Nature moves in natural ways. It grows and changes. It connects to other parts of nature that are growing and changing. Roots of trees share water when it's dry. Leaves fall when the weather turns cold. Blooms return in the spring when the sun warms the earth again and the cycles start all over.

That is the same for our human lives.

The Element of the North

In the North we are resting and replenishing our soil. We are letting our old leaves shed.

In the East we are moving out of winter, and we change and can create new blooms in our lives, planting seeds of possibility in our minds.

In the South we are allowing our spiritual gifts and our wants and needs to add sunlight to the seeds we've planted.

In the West we water our soil, our seeds, and our desires and put them in motion.

We are as natural as nature.

This vast wisdom and awareness can be found in nature. Wisdom can also be found in the soil that holds the remains of the millions of humans who lived before us and were buried in the ground we walk on. The remains of every human buried or burned are now part of the soil that we all call home. We walk and live on their human graves. How many days of our lives go by where we forget that our home and the nature around us also carry the physical remnants of thousands of years of other humans (not to mention animals).

Earth is the foundation of our lives, as it is both our home and our source of sustenance. The Earth element is ever-present and highly versatile, manifesting as both soil and seed, and witnessed in the eternal rhythms of growth, harvest, decay, and regeneration.

Earth carries a natural vibration; through rituals and spells we become aligned with the natural order of things. We cannot bypass the natural order of things, even in spell work.

Earth is represented by the diverse topographical features found all over the planet, including forests, fields, caves, rocks, valleys, and gardens. This "classical" element in witchcraft is associated with abundance, prosperity, and strength.

Not only is the earth the source and sustainer of plant and animal life, but it has also provided the clay and minerals with which humans have made tools, and the trees and stone we've used to build our homes and other structures. Earth's energy also has a destructive side, which may be experienced as earthquakes, avalanches, or mudslides. Our own unprocessed emotions also have a destructive side.

The natural disasters as we call them are less natural and more a result of how the planet Earth has changed due to our own mismanagement of resources, which has led to climate change. This book is not about climate change as a whole, but I would be remiss if I didn't remind you right here and right now that we humans are the force behind the increase in natural disasters in the world. Do your own research (even looking back hundreds of years), and you'll find that, yes, planet Earth has a destructive side that is natural but you'll also find it is increasing at a rapid pace because of the human race.

We can look at how our planet has very angry moments and shakes and quivers, see how increased rain seasons lead to flooding, and watch fires that burn large acres in many countries, and we can wonder what the endgame of all this ongoing change is.

We can look at these angry moments of the planet and ask ourselves questions.

> **Earth:** When were you so angry that you wanted to bang your fists on the table and rage? That is unbalanced feelings inside our body that want to be expressed through movement. The unbalanced feelings in our body are unbalanced resources.

The Element of the North

Air: When did you last feel rejected then spew a stream of words at the next person who crossed your path because your mind was actually hurting, but it came out sideways at anyone in your path? That is unbalanced thoughts that didn't have an outlet to be moved. Our words spew when they don't have a healthy outlet to move.

Fire: When have you held back your true wants and set them aside to care for others first and adopted the role of people pleasing until one day they erupted like a volcano and spewed hot lava on everyone? Fire needs a way to move, and if we do not give it space to do so, it will build and build and then explode—more unbalanced resources.

Water: Have you held back your emotions out of fear of being judged as being too emotional or crying over something small and keeping it trapped inside? When you do so, it will come raging out of you another way and will create a tidal wave of change in your life. It's often not the way we want change to happen, but it becomes too much to hold the emotions back, and they come out in destructive ways like a tidal wave.

Because our body and nature are alike, any unbalanced or unregulated feelings, thoughts, desires, or emotions that are repressed will come out and create destruction. Just as Mother Nature does.

Witch work includes knowing how to connect to the earth at any time for wisdom, substance, or grounding, and casting spells with the cooperation of earth energy. Witch work is also honoring our planet and everything in nature and treating it as sacred.

A few ways you can work toward creating sacredness with nature are to plant new seeds every time you harvest plants, pick up trash and plastics in your neighborhood, recycle everything you can including natural items (like wood), purchase recycled goods, study plants and trees in your neighborhood, plant new trees, work with environmental organizations that support new growth, and balance your consumption. The list is endless, yet if we all start small in our own little stretch of home, the world would be a different place.

Also pay the same amount of attention to your body and notice where you consume waste and aren't tending to your own garden (your life and relationships). One leads to the other, and when you tend to your life as the garden of all possibilities, it will grow and flourish.

You need not call yourself a witch to do this work; the label doesn't matter—what matters is the choice to use earth as a source of medicine.

Take a moment and look around you. Really look, no matter where you are when you read this. Notice anything made of wood? Real wood. Furniture, houses, structures, utensils. Notice all of it. Then close your eyes and picture all that wood as a tree before it was cut down. And that tree might have been big when it was cut, but picture it as a baby tree. Then a single sapling and then further back even to when it was a seed fallen from another tree and landing in the soil. That one seed could have produced everything you see made of wood.

That's sacred magic.

The earth element can combine with water, absorb it, or be carved out by it, depending on the amount of each element. The same can essentially be said of its relationship with fire and air.

This is the same as how our own bodies react with the other elements. When we soak in the water, we feel weightless and can carve out the space in the water with our body (freedom and flow). When our body is combined with fire, we can transmute (change) or destruct (anger). Our body combined with air is powerful and free (choice).

Let's now explore the basic spiritual and magical associations with earth. The earth is feminine; she is the goddess and is a receptive energy. Traditional tools in spiritual practices are the pentacle, sacred geometric shapes, salt, water;

and all living plants and trees. Her magical colors are any color associated with her natural elements.

Traditional magic uses salt as a symbol of earth. A circle on the earth is often used as a source of protection before casting spells or rituals, such as arranging a circle of rocks around you while sitting outside for magic or meditation, or drawing a circle in the sand while at the beach. We can make natural circles for magic whenever we are outside in nature.

Soil and most plants can be added to magical charms or be used to cleanse crystals and other tools. Many spells call for burying biodegradable objects in the earth; for example, using a plant on your altar and returning it to the earth when you've finished with it. Or when you have written in your journal focusing on releasing old versions of you, then you bury the writing.

Any items foraged in nature, whether living or dried, are represented by the earth. This means the list of what can be used from nature for magical purposes is virtually endless. The earth is associated with your body, skin, being grounded and rooted, connecting to people and plants, your ancestors, community, stability, fertility, stillness, patience, sluggishness, and lethargy.

Let's take a moment to talk about grounding. You have likely heard this word mentioned a time or two and might not know exactly what it means or how to do it. Although there are many ways to do grounding rituals, the simplest way is to imagine the earth as one giant ball of energy that beats to a slow heartbeat. The heartbeat feels like a deep breath, and when you are in nature, you can let that deep, slow pulse of energy travel through your body and relax you. You can feel this simply by stepping outside with bare feet or finding a patch of grass or dirt to let the bottom of your feet soak in the energy. If it's winter, you can walk and breathe the cool air into your lungs. Connect any part of you, inside your lungs or any surface area of your skin, with something natural outdoors. That's how you ground.

You need more earth element when you are always on the go and find it hard doing nothing or you cannot be in stillness. Or if you are disconnected from your body. Or even times when you are processing deep feelings such as stress, anxiety, fear, or depression. These are times to practice grounding.

To balance these times of not enough connection, add more earth. Start by spending time literally on the ground. In most seasons you can sit, lie, or walk barefoot. A little rain or a little cold will not hurt you if it's only for a few minutes. Hold long yoga poses to align more with your body. Add in self-massage, touching your scalp or even flower/plant brushing. You are also craving the earth element when you want more physical contact with loved ones. Hugs, snuggles, or even a shoulder pat are a connection. Skin to skin is earth magic. You can sleep naked or tend a garden and/or houseplants. Eat more fruits and vegetables. Whiff or rub essential oils such as sandalwood, juniper, cedar, balsam, or vetiver on your body.

Most of the time when we do not have enough earth element, it is also a sign that we need to slow down and rest. In today's busy world of nonstop activities and nonstop scrolling, almost everyone needs more time in the North with the element of earth.

You have excess earth element when you feel heavy and weighed down. You always feel behind and unmotivated to start projects. You feel lazy or heavy, spiritually or physically. You feel like you are patient and accepting, but often we are unmotivated to make a change or to add more fire to the situation.

To balance having too much earth, add more fire by moving your body and sweating. Practice chanting, the breath of fire, or dancing. Hike, drum, or meditate by connecting to your heartbeat. Use chanting combined with movement for a fast change of heaviness. You can also bring in the element of water to lighten your energy.

Anytime you feel out of alignment, the earth can bring balance and restore your connection to yourself. Exploring the connection to yourself is a sacred ritual and is the purest of magic that exists. To do this, though, means knowing when you are not in alignment or when you are slightly off. Regardless of the reason, the earth holds the medicine you need. Every single time.

The Element of the North

When you study magic, you are studying transformation. When you study transformation, you will embark on a journey deep into the core of yourself. The deeper you sink into yourself and feel how you, a human in an ecosystem on this planet, are connected to the earth, the more the magic reveals itself in the cycles all around you. When you see the cycles, know them and how they impact you, then begin to add in rituals (like those in Part Two of this book), and everything you know life to be now will change. Colors will get brighter every time you step outside. You'll smell the scents of the earth deeper when you bring the connection into your body and clear out old, stuck energy. You will also feel so much more alive, and when this happens, you will taste the long-awaited freedom. Longing for freedom is what we do when we step into nature with purpose and intention. Sacred magic will be found when you spend time connecting to nature as part of your daily rituals and habits.

Contemplation questions

1. The last time I felt connected to nature was?

2. What did I just learn about the element of earth that I know I want to practice more of?

3. How many minutes or hours have I allowed myself time in nature with no electronic or communication device in the last seven days? In the last thirty days?

4. If nature is the path to my own magic, how would I arrange my schedule to allow for more time in nature?

5. Why have I not prioritized myself and my time in nature?

6. Do I have too much or too little of earth at the moment? How can I create balance?

Chapter Four
Plant Allies of the North

𝒫LANTS ARE ALLIES, as they contain their own unique spiritual and physical properties that can be both medicine and energy neutralizers, and they can interact with our own human energy. Plants produce an element we humans must have in order to survive—oxygen. Plants are our allies due to the fact that we can breathe because of them, we can have a healthy body from eating them and they grow constantly and bring us joy.

When you think of plants, I want you to think bigger than the one you are struggling to keep alive on your windowsill. The plant category encompasses flowers, vegetables, vines, indoor and outdoor plants, wild or cultivated species, and dried plants for teas and herbs, plus those burned for smoke clearing and used as decoration and for protection from the wind. Plants are where essential oils and ingredients come from.

When I ask you to think bigger, I mean think of the hundreds of thousands of plant species there are on our planet and know that each one has a separate physical and spiritual property (or energetic imprint). Plants are as different as we are as humans.

Wow, right? Welcome to plants as allies.

As we move deeper and deeper into the connection between the earth and our body, we must spend time in the North looking at specific plants and how they can create spiritual, physical, and mental changes in our lives. The difference between a plant just being a plant that you don't even notice and a plant that is your ally is your choice to connect with it and work directly with all facets of the plant's energy.

There was one occasion where I utilized a plant as a way to connect with different worlds, and it completely changed the outcome of the ritual I had planned.

It started when I planned a ceremony to be conducted outdoors under the moon at a place I had rented in New Mexico. It was on a large property and had space for an outdoor fire and a place to paint afterward as I like to do. I selected this location as it's known for being a powerful energy center that could hold the magic I was about to weave. It was a ceremony of death and rebirth. I planned this ceremony to let the old versions of me be shed to make way for the new. It was to be an honoring of all the ways I felt fear of being seen and being judged.

I was responding to a calling deep in my body to work with magic. I was at a place in my first business where people knew me as an international nonprofit business expert. I had also opened the mystery school but had kept these communities separate. My podcast and public work had been focused on the field of business, and my podcast was intended to support women who were also striving to overcome obstacles emanating from the sheer fact of being a woman. Simultaneously, I was also committed to my body's health and pursued competitive weight lifting and had trained for years in a form of self-defense called Krav Maga as both a student and eventually a teacher.

I kept them all separate and felt parts of myself segregated into the various versions of me that showed up with the part of me that was needed in each moment. I kept my nature witch work separate from the shamanic drumming I did in another circle. I kept my fellow fitness professionals separate from the embodiment work I did after dark to heal my sore muscles. I didn't talk about the rituals I did in my car on the way to teach self-defense or the protection magic tools I used to ward off the need for physical violence in self-defense. I led business meetings not talking about the sigils I had on the top of the agenda that would create better communication in the meeting. I was living multiple lives in the same life.

I did this because I carried fear that I would be judged across *all* the communities I was a part of. If several of the nonprofit organizations that were funded by religious institutions I worked with found out I was a witch, it could impact the their funding. Or if my fitness friends found out a part of my healing included deep work with plant allies, I might be labeled a little crazy. What if my weight-lifting colleagues discovered I invoked land spirits during competitions to help me avoid injuries? The fear of judgment was real, and I carried it inside me for a very long time.

I also knew that several of the spiritual communities I was in carried judgment about capitalism, and following traditional business practices was frowned on, yet my businesses were built with traditional business principles. There was a minefield of judgment all around me at all times—or so I thought. I was torn and only a part of me was present in each area of my life out of fear of this judgment.

I wanted to begin finding ways to be my full self in all areas of my life and put an end to the fragments of me that were visible only to certain people at certain times.

The merging of all parts of me began when I started contemplating changing my podcast to spiritual and witchcraft topics, adding my magical truths to my social media. It was a small step, but at the time it felt huge. It was a craving to be seen as my whole self, magic and all. I wanted the wholeness of who I had become to be in one body, rooted in the fact that I was and am all these parts of me.

This desire to merge all my parts was the ceremony I had planned. It was to support the transition of who I had been *into* who I was becoming.

To aid me in the death of separateness, I had decided to take a baby plant I had been growing for weeks with me. This baby plant was the plant of death, as each part of the plant was poisonous. The plant was a belladonna, an ancient plant in a witch's arsenal. It has been used for thousands of years by witches. I think that's what fascinated me at the time, growing something that was illegal in some states and had the capacity to take a human life.

I am extremely adept at feeling into the energetic properties of plants. I have been this way since I was young (as you will be after reading this book). I could feel my Belladonna's power from the moment I said yes to growing it. When collecting supplies for my ceremony, she was beaming at me to take her with me.

I packed her in her pot and brought her for the journey to the home I had rented. When I arrived to unpack my supplies, I set her down with some other indoor plants to rest a while before I proceeded.

I resumed the ritual, completing the rites of death and rebirth, and I connected with Belladonna the entire time.

I took the whole plant, dirt and all, and held it in both hands during the part of the ceremony where I lay still and allowed the working I did to settle into my body. The belladonna was like holding my finger in an electrical socket. It supercharged my entire body, and she came awake when tasked with aiding my own spiritual death so I could be reborn into the new version of me that wanted to be set free.

The vibration of holding her in my hand imparted an energy that even now I can close my eyes and call upon anytime. She was powerful.

When the ceremony was done, I packed her back in her pot and returned home. I gave her blessings and thanked her for aiding me. When I woke up after I had returned home, I was shocked to see the entire plant was dead. Not just wilting or tilting to one side, but completely dead, as if it had been sitting there unwatered for months—that's how dead she was. I was sad for a moment as this plant is not only hard to grow, but I had become so fond of her. I had taken the seed and infused it and made magic with her growth. She had been instrumental in the transformational experience during the ceremony I had just completed. I felt a kinship with this small plant and felt grief that she had left so easily. I wondered if I had caused her death, if it was a type of sacrifice in my ceremony.

It may seem silly or a waste of grief to feel this for a small plant. But as a witch who connects deeply to plants and can feel their energy, I definitely felt it like a loss. I remained curious about it for days after. Or maybe I was truly just curious about the amount of time in my life I had wasted worrying about judgment and I released it all in one single ritual.

A few days later I was sitting near where the energy of the belladonna plant remained even though its growth had died, and I was painting on a fresh canvas, creating a visual of the experience I had had. I began to receive a message from Belladonna. She said she had completed her purpose. She grew from day one knowing she would aid me in my own ceremony of death and her work was now complete. She had grown for a single purpose and that purpose had been achieved—to show me my own truth and let the truths that were really just fear of judgment be seen and then easily die.

I stopped my painting and grabbed a smaller brush and wrote her name on the painting with an expression of gratitude. This painting, even today, carries the feeling of death and rebirth following the message from Belladonna. She showed me how easily we can let old beliefs just die.

I use plants in all ceremonies and rituals. I drink tea blends that create an energetic shift in my field, I sleep with certain plants when I want to expand my dreams or remember them, and I smell each plant, fruit, and vegetable before I consume it. It's amazing to connect with plants in all facets of life, not to mention in sacred practices.

When I spent time in Hawaii, I was introduced to native plants that I worked with while I called the lands "home" during my stay. When in the mountains writing, I foraged for wildflowers. When I moved to the island on the East Coast where I live now, I found myself drawn to certain flowers and blooms that I like to wear in my hair as an honoring of how special it is for them to grow in a saltwater environment.

Plants, trees, and all things that grow, wild or tamed, are energetic connections. When you learn to view plants as a source of deeper connection to all living things, the magical ways in which you choose to walk among them will change. The natural world goes beyond using plants as herbal remedies, although we'll do that, too. Instead, it's the inherent wisdom in nature that I want to introduce you to in this chapter.

In all the directions and included in each book in this series is a section on the power of plant allies. I know you might expect witch work to be hovering over a cauldron and adding chicken bones and speaking in rhyme—and it can be—but the living embodiment of witch work is the daily practices and rituals we do that create constant magical connections throughout our daily lives. We can use plants to enchant our clothes before we put them on, to wash away our stress at the end of the day, and to write our deepest secrets on and let nature put them into motion. That's real witch work and is the core of daily sacred magic.

All plants are born of the North, and in traditional practices you'll see most people classify them as the element of earth. When we walk the spiral path of magic, we find that there are different plants that will journey with us in each direction.

Plant Allies of the North

North: Plants to the North support our journey inward to deeper levels of connection to our body and support our never-ending death and rebirth cycles. Barley, Beet, Cotton, Fern, Mugwort, Rhubarb, and Wheat.

East: Plants to the East know how to highlight where our beliefs are skewed and where our voice is stunted and also how to aid us in journeying out and back into our body. Anise, Dandelion, Lavender, Marjoram, Mint, Parsley, and Sage.

South: Plants to the South awaken deep levels of sovereignty, passion, and ancient wisdom. Allspice, Bay, Clove, Cumin, Dill, Frankincense, Nutmeg, Onion, and Pepper.

West: Plants to the West remind us of our fluidity in all things and how to move with the earth's waters. Blackberry, Cabbage, Cucumber, Daffodil, Jasmine, Poppy, and Vanilla.

My approach is to teach you how to use the diversity and interconnectedness of all plant life as a way to see the interconnectedness inside of us and how to bring them into your life with intention, both the living forms of nature and the spiritual representations of them. It is a slow and steady process of adding the magic of plants into your life and your body, one at a time and with intention.

If you are feeling overwhelmed and so busy that you don't know how to slow down, increase the amount of salads you are eating and add a healthy dose of beet greens. Use mugwort as a tea to slow down and help rest. Spend more time tending to a single plant in your home with thought and intention.

When your words feel bottled up and you are having a hard time speaking truth, combine lavender essential oil with mint on your palms, rub them together, and breathe them in deeply. Burn dried sage to move stagnant energy.

If you want to move energy and create more momentum or action for a particular goal or project, add allspice and cloves to your coffee or food.

If you feel too much stress or inflexibility and want to bring in more flow, drink a blackberry leaf tea, sprinkle the leaf into your dinner, or take deep breaths of jasmine essential oil.

Every plant and tree—from a towering oak that feels like it's the grandmother of the land to a humble dandelion we work so hard to rid our yards of—offers a uniquely magical signature that coincides with intentions, emotions, and symbolic attributes. Just as Belladonna did with my death and rebirth. Everything in the natural world is an active participant in creation. We can find our own power of persistence, just as we would in a weed that grows between the cracks of the sidewalk. Its wisdom can teach us our own persistence. You can feel the vibrations of the lands when you attune to a plant. A plant can feel you when you attune to it. It feels the life in you and can respond in turn to the life you wish to create that feels sacred and magical to you.

You can give and receive energy when you attune to a plant, as I did with Belladonna. They have a remarkable and steadfast capacity to absorb energy, to infuse us back, and to hold our greatest emotion for us.

Reading this, you may wonder why you haven't used plants as allies before now.

If you've bought fresh flowers on a holiday or occasion, you've been using the energy of plants as a gift (plant magic). Or if you've planted a garden or planted blooms at your front door, you've created welcoming energy. You may tend to your lawn with loving care or stop to smell the jasmine when blooming in the spring; that's connecting to the energy of plants. You might have sent flowers to someone for a special occasion or when someone has passed; in truth, the plants themselves will help energetically with the grief process.

Plants heal. They brighten space and bring life to it. They represent beauty, steadfastness, and love. Plants also teach you how easy it is to grow and change, and that it's natural to do so.

Plant Allies of the North

We can tame them to fit inside our dwellings and they will grow and bless our space with aliveness. We can witness them wild outdoors in wonderment and ask ourselves where we desire to be wilder. All and everything we feel we can find in a plant.

I teach many rituals that start with seeds that we infuse with our intentions and wishes then release them somewhere in the wild where our intentions can come to fruition. You can do this too anytime you are planting new seeds. You can start by opening the packet and holding the seeds in your hands. Imagine what they will grow into and why you are planting them. You can add them to a small bowl and put your fingers in them several times a day with a blessing of gratitude that they will grow just for you. If you have any intentions or goals in your life at the time, write them down and slip them under the bowl of seeds.

The results of infusing seeds with your energy and intentions are powerful, and it always works to enhance the seeds' growth and the growth in your life. (See Part Two of this book for many other rituals for you to bring into your practice.)

We can collect plants during a walk and bring them home as a reminder of the freedom to move amid nature. The saying "stop and smell the roses" is a true mantra of being in the North.

Slow down and let the plants you find change you. Breathe them in. Watch a bee take nectar from a plant and carry it to another. Look at the colors of the entire rainbow that can be found in blooms. Talk to the plants and you will find that the plants will start to talk back. Smell leaves of a tree and you'll be very surprised at how different they smell. Taking their scent into your body will be like bringing in a breath of fresh sunlight.

Next time you take a walk or are even walking from the grocery store to your car, find a tree and a leaf or part of the bark that is exposed and rub it with your fingers and smell the tree. Look at the shapes of the branches and the leaves. When you gaze at and take in the essence of a tree, your entire body feels it and will naturally calm your nervous system. This is magic and can be done every time you pass a tree, although it may make for a long walk if there are many trees along the way. The experience is so enlightening that you won't want to stop (even if people wonder what is happening while you are smelling a tree in the parking lot of a grocery store). Whisper thank you when you are done with the tree.

Trees in groupings such as a large forest have interconnected roots and will share water with those that receive less, just as we live in community with our friends and family and share love when others feel less. We are born with the same longings as the trees—to be connected and watered when we feel low.

Plants will shed their leaves naturally to make space for new growth, just as we shed versions of ourselves in order to grow. I can guarantee that when you look at your life so far, you can see how different you are now compared to ten or twenty years ago. So can a plant or tree. It's all connected and it's all sacred.

In winter months plants go into a deep rest and appear dead, just as with us when we are deep into the underworld or when we spend time in the North. They need rest from growing toward the sun or from blooming, or they need to let their blooms die so their roots get stronger. So do we.

Spending time in nature is a critical step in connecting to yourself and learning how energy in nature impacts your own energy. This can be any type of nature: the snowy days when you know the earth is sleeping beneath your feet, the spring awakening with tiny signs of life that bring such joy, the summer when everything is slightly wilted under the heat of the sun, or the cool days of fall. We can find ourselves in each of these seasons, no matter where we live, whether surrounded by a forest or just a tree or two at a local park.

The magic of plants can be brought forth no matter the season, as you can work with them in dried forms, seed forms, drawings—all of these will create an energetic connection, even if the earth is sleeping.

Nature has a unique way of grounding us and connecting us to our true selves. Each season offers its own magic and lessons. Winter teaches us the beauty of rest and introspection, spring fills us with hope and new beginnings, summer encourages us to embrace abundance and growth, and autumn reminds us of the importance of letting go. By attuning ourselves to these natural rhythms, we align more closely with the inner cycles of life itself.

Grounding is a practice used to release any energy that has created a wobble in your center. Whether it's expansive magical workings that leave you feeling like you are floating in the cosmos, deep anger that you are unable to express, or anything in between, grounding helps stabilize you. When we are not grounded, all our actions, thoughts, and beliefs can become skewed.

When I need grounding before performing a spell or ritual to ensure I have focused and balanced emotions, I use breathwork or plant brushing. Plant brushing is an easy go-to for plant magic. Find a small part of a plant that you can cut or forage (or buy if it's off-season) and run the leaves or blooms of the plant along your bare skin, all of your skin, then return the plant to nature. It will remove energy and recharge you.

Grounding and centering outdoors among the plants is always going to be the fastest and most effective way to relieve stress or big emotions. Grounding is how you center and balance any part of your mind, body, or spirit that is leaning too heavily one way. Even in inclement weather, going outdoors to smell the fresh air and feel the cycles that nature in your area is currently in is quick and easy. The natural world provides a powerful, ever-present source of grounding energy, as it is the energy of all plants and trees. It reconnects us to our roots and helps us find stability amid the chaos of daily life.

Plants you will consume, such as natural teas, infusions, and remedies, should only be undertaken if you are working with an experienced practitioner or after doing extensive research first. I make teas with plants daily and have checked them all thoroughly both with an herbalist and my medical practitioner. I suggest you do the same. I will include a few recipes and ways to consume a plant, but know yourself first and take caution. Make sure you research them thoroughly. A daily infusion with tea is a life-changing practice, as the plant will come into your body and heal any deficiencies and provide a heavy amount of minerals and vitamins.

Another magical and powerful way to work with plants as allies is for protection magic. Creating talismans, sachets, and sacred smoke with sage, mugwort, and cedar can create a protective barrier against unwanted energy—from yourself and your own inner voice and also from others. Plants can protect your energy and your body from illness and can help you fill in the gaps where you lack the emotional or physical strength to do so yourself.

Plants are also great diviners and can share wisdom on the journey inward. They can magnify your intentions if you are working on prosperity, love, and growth. Flowers, blooms, and greenery are easy to source and easy to use. Forage for what's around you and hold it. Write your questions on it and sit with that piece of nature. There are entire universes of historical knowledge available in each plant if you ask and listen. Foraging, sitting with the plants, and writing on them can all be their own ritual and spell work that is easy to do anytime and anyplace. You do not have to call yourself a nature witch to work with the magic of plants.

While we are in the North, we also need to consider the root of the plants. Roots that remain under the soil can be harvested for the times you feel buried in the soil, stuck, or unable to find your way out of the darkness. Roots can be used in shadow work, rituals, and spells that will aid you in getting to the bottom of any questions you may have. They can also be used when you are exploring what you want next in life and can allow you time to build a foundational connection to plants as allies.

I personally grow and work with several poisonous plants that I bring into my practice when I am teaching students how to cut energetic cords, such as holding a plant in your hands while doing rituals to allow relationships to end or when you are leaving a job. Always use caution when working with poisonous plants but know that their energy is powerful.

Often when I'm teaching or doing protection magic, I'll put a bloom of oleander in my hair to aid me in my strength as a warrior. For this reason, I call oleander the "death mother," my own personal nickname for her, as I have used her in many ways, and I feel her energy as a slow and loving death to any situation I want changed or if I'm calling in protection for myself or someone else. I also journey with Belladonna when I am holding space for others' trauma, and we are journeying into the underworld. Belladonna is a powerful ally when fighting the shadows and I consider her one of my greatest tools. I grow her, harvest her, and let her rest in the winter months.

My home contains more than fifty indoor plants that I feel deeply; I feel the fresh, alive energy they fill my space with. My outdoor gardens grow wild and free to remind me I am free to grow in wild ways. I have entire bookshelves of dried herbs that I am not able to grow that I keep for magical and connective purposes. I keep a jar of bay leaves at all times to do quick rituals, as they are easy to write on with a marker to release a thought or emotion that isn't serving me (especially if I am looping in a bubble of worry about something I cannot control), then I burn the whole thing. I have several jars of dried plants, such as dried lavender and frankincense, that I burn on an incense disc to create an immediate uplifting of spirits. If I want to aid my psychic work or am preparing to use dreamtime as time for insight, I'll burn dragon's blood resin or myrrh resin.

With their intrinsic ties to physical and spiritual properties, plants in each direction hold a significant amount of wisdom. I will include a short list to get you started, but keep in mind, working with local plants that are native to your lands is more important than any of the commonly used ones I share.

Before you embark on working with plants as allies, I want you to consider them as living and breathing facets of our planet. When you harvest, talk to, work with, or change any plant or tree, take a moment to connect with the plant and ask its permission. Trust the first answer that comes to you. Never take all the blooms when cutting them from outdoors as that is over-consuming, and we need only a small amount, and you should leave a few behind.

As a nature-dwelling witch, I often find myself wanting to bring a small piece of a plant home to study it or add it to my altar. At least thirty percent of the time when I ask the plant for permission, I hear a strong "no," and I say thank you and carry on. Listen to the plants.

Always leave something in place of something you've taken. It can be a strand of hair, a little drink of your water, or your gentle voice in song. The plant appreciates your offering and will naturally open its energy to you deeper.

If you live in a city or location where nature is hard to find, consider exploring local parks and green spaces. They can always be found, even if they're man-made. Sit or walk in the space on a regular basis, observe the wildlife, touch the living parts of nature, and thank it for being a sanctuary. It always amplifies your connection when you take a few minutes to journal on what you felt.

Make nature your cathedral at least once a month by finding a place to sit and rest. Contemplate your time in the North and how your body feels. Work the questions at the end of the chapter during this sacred time. Let the forests be the sentinels along the path of your life.

When you add plants and trees into your life as allies and use your connection to them in your daily practice, I can promise you that what you will begin to experience in your life will be so transformative that you'll feel the deep call of remembering your magic. You can start with one plant ally at a time and exchange energy with it to experience what is possible with natural energy.

The plants and trees will show you their makeup by how it feels in your body to touch them, smell them, and feel them. They will help you when you are seeking big or small life changes or contemplating what you want out of this life by infusing you with life-force energy that is always at your fingertips just by going outside.

Contemplation questions

1. My favorite flower bloom is?

2. The plants that most often hold my attention are?

3. What can I grow now, indoors or outdoors, that I would love to know more about?

4. If I could ask a plant to help me process one thing I'm facing right now, what would I ask?

Chapter Five
Your Body Is the North

Your soul is the essence of you in a combination of your personality and your spirit, and it is housed inside your body. The soul is housed inside your body for a short time called life, where it can experience all the amazing and the hard parts of being a human. The soul of each of us is a bridge between the mundane human worlds and the great big energy force we've called many things (god, goddess, universe, consciousness). If our soul comes from the great big energy force of god and is ready to come down into the earthly place and experience humanness, we do so for a specific reason, and that reason is to be experienced in our body.

Another way to think of it is our soul (or our spirit) is a ball of energy, a bright pulsing light like a star in the sky. It is an energy that holds wisdom, experiences, and traits that are present only for that bright light. When that bright light moves itself into a human body at birth, all memory of where it came from is erased in order to have a real, full, human experience.

Since we come from the light and will return to the light, for the small time in between skin, flesh, bones, and each cell inside holds our soul in the temporary home to the bright light of who we truly are. We choose this body before we come here as our temporary house for the lifetime of experiences, almost as if when we were a bright ball of energy, we hovered over a shopping list of what we wanted to experience when we dropped into a human body. We choose our parents, we choose our skin and body shape, and we choose who is going to come along for the bumpy as well as the fun parts of the ride, and who is coming along from the spiritual realm to support us. We choose to create a bucket list of experiences as a rough outline of what we'll do while human. We take an item from the list that will be our main functioning center and add it to our human experience and call it a brain. The brain is the filter for processing and is also the place that holds the mind. We also choose a heart from the list, one that will be in charge of pumping blood through our body for aliveness and will also hold the energy of love. Each organ we choose will have a function of use in our temporary house, and it also holds an energetic use. Our eyes will be the functioning tool that deciphers what we need to know as a human and will also connect to both our brain and our mind and will emit information into our soul at all times. This is the same with all five senses: They will hold functional human needs as well as being a bridge between our soul that is housed inside our flesh. Our soul will talk to us and emit information to our human selves through our senses, feelings, and heart every second of the time we are human.

When we die, our soul will gather each experience, lesson, and moment of love and take them back with it when it returns to a ball of light. The system of tallying up each of our human experiences was built into the body in miraculous ways and will hold the memories, experiences, and entirety of the soul's experience inside our cells and body.

The soul is alive inside our body, and our senses are working and feeding information to and from the soul. Our organs will process the physical part of our human body and will also digest our feelings and experiences. Our heart will work to keep us alive and is continually beating inside our chest; even while you are reading this, your heart is working very hard to pump blood to all parts of your body. The miracle that happens when you pause and think about this is you can actually feel your heart beating. You can feel your heart working to keep you alive regardless of what you are doing in the moment. Yet how many minutes, hours, and days go by without a second thought to the magic going on inside of us to keep us alive?

Our body is both the place that houses our soul and the place that all experiences go as tallies of what we've experienced.

We make these decisions when we are still a bright ball of light until it's time to go into our human form. I always imagine what the clock might look like when you are a ball of light and it's time to be born into a body, and I wonder if it's a full countdown like a New Year's Eve clock—3, 2, 1, whoosh, off we go!

When it's time to drop into our body, we throw the list and all this knowledge away and hold onto one final piece of wisdom from the time we were a bright ball of light, and that's *free will*. We will have free will once we become human and will get to choose once we are on planet Earth. When we are there and riding the ride of humanness, we maintain free will with our power to *choose*. We choose and track each choice inside our body. Whoosh, our memory of being only a ball of light goes away and the next thing we know, we are inside a tiny human body, and it's cold outside our mother's womb, and we cry for safety.

While you're reading this now, it's unlikely that you remember your birth the days you learned to walk, or each milestone when you were young. Your brain may not remember it, but your body does. In fact, every experience you have had so far in life has been put through the filter of your mind to decide if it's one that stays in the front of the memories or if it's one you will bury in order to not experience it again. When our mind makes the decision to bury something and we push it deep into our brain, it doesn't go away; it remains dormant and hidden. It's buried in what we call the shadows. Even though our mind has moved it to a secret place in order to avoid it, our body has stored it somewhere inside our physical being, and it remains there. No matter the feelings associated with it, joy or pain, it stays inside the body. If our body builds up too much of the shadow feelings that are hidden from our mind, our body will become sick and diseased from too much pain or experiences we want to avoid. Our body also holds the joy and love we have had along the way, and these experiences become the antidote to parts we keep hidden.

The only way out of the state of the built-up darkness that our body holds is to actually be in our body and feel it, acknowledge it, move it out, and replace it with more joy and more love. Your mind can (and will) keep a catalog of these memories without them being hidden or locked down, and the memories themselves can be neutralized from any feeling by moving them out of your body. You can do this by *choosing* what you want to store in your body and *choosing* to let what you don't want stored in your body be moved out.

Our physical body carries every single experience we've had as an energetic imprint inside our cells that can be identified and seen as clearly as the growth lines on the leaf of a plant. This imprint lives in our organs, tissue, and skin: The stress, the joy, the fear, and all of the in between live in our cells. The stress we've experienced is stored like an old forgotten apple left at the bottom of the fridge for months until it turns shrunken and moldy, constantly there, emitting moldy energy into our body.

Any chance of experiencing joy will be drowned out if all we feel are rotten apples.

Your Body Is the North

Joy, like a refreshing breeze, has the power to clear away the stagnant energy of past wounds. As we embrace more joy and heal these old scars, our body transforms into a sanctuary of comfort and confidence. We can then connect to each movement of our body with newfound freedom. This liberation allows us to offer ourselves the most precious gift—the gift of our body becoming a channel for our senses to experience more of our soul's truest desires.

It's magical how our body's connection to our senses and our soul brings a profound sense of presence to every moment when we learn how to see that's it's all connected. When we listen through our ears, we are fully immersed in that vibrant moment that is experienced in waves of sound that we interpret based on our experiences of that sound in our life. When we feel the softness of a blanket against our skin, we are reminded that our skin is a gigantic organ that loves to feel itself by experiencing new tangible ways of being touched and doing the touching. When we gaze at nature through our eyes, our senses are heightened, and we are not lost in thoughts of the past or future. We are fully present in that beautiful, fleeting slice of time, and it's the closest we come to the feeling of once being a ball of light and how peaceful is.

If the old moldy apple is still inside of us, joy will be felt through the stench of rotting. Our senses will be deciphered differently from the shadows we hid in our brain that our body has stored and will block our ability to feel real levels of joy and love. Even when we try to hide the shadows, it's no different than putting a towel over the rotten apple in the fridge and pretending it's not there. It's still there; it's just temporarily out of view. We cannot process any of the feelings of the greatest parts of being human if we don't clear out the rotten apples and connect deeply to how our body has stored and tallied all our life experiences.

One easy way to begin to loosen the hold of what we store is movement. Movement shakes it all up and loosens it so we can move the old moldy bits and refresh our cells. Movement will show you where your muscles hold tension, which brings aches and pains into our joints. Movement that moves energy can be any type of exercise, including walking, dancing, and yoga flows.

You may know only where your body hurts or is sore, that you feel unwell or unmotivated, you cannot sleep, or you have any number of other ailments. You might not know that the primary reason, meaning the underlying reason behind the symptom, is energetic more often than not. By energetic, I mean our body is still holding as energy all of these stored experiences that we push away into the back of our mind and try to pretend are not there. Another way to say it is that unfelt emotions, unprocessed negative experiences, all the parts we keep in the shadows become trapped energy inside every single aspect of our physical being, and they cause physical pain and disease (dis-ease) in our body.

Looking into and at our body, really looking, takes courage and the perspective of why we came here in the first place. Because so much of our physical body is replicated in nature, we must look to nature to aid us in the brave quest to understand our body, what it has stored, and why. Because nature is the closest we can find to the connection to our soul, it is the most powerful way to explore this work.

Our body is made up of energy, both positive and negative, which impacts how we access our inner spiritual selves (our soul). Once we see and feel that energy is ever present in all parts of us, we can learn to move the energy in the direction that matches what our soul desires.

Here is a simple way to start, right here and right now: Wherever you are reading this, take a moment to close your eyes and focus your attention on your feet. Are they comfortable and resting, do they hurt, or are they balancing your connection to the ground?

Then move up into your hips; Pause a moment and take a deep breath and feel into your hips. How do they feel right now?

Then move to your belly, your chest, your shoulders, your neck, your face, and your arms. What do you feel? Where is there tension and where is there ease?

What you have just done in a short time is bring full presence to your body right now. This is just the beginning of our work connecting to our body. Clearing out the old, stagnant parts and increasing the amount of joy we experience are essential parts of the spiral path of magic. If we want more magic and to spiral through the elements of all parts of our life, that joy is the emotion we are questing for.

We start **in the North** with this book because our body is an essential component of understanding ourselves. When we study magic, we study transformation. Our body is miraculous and can and will transform in our lifetime; the question is if we are choosing to transform it for the betterment of our lives.

When we move **to the East** and the element of air, we will do the same process, but we'll do it in the beautiful space we call our mind. Our mind is what holds our beliefs and thoughts. These beliefs and thoughts, like a filter, directly impact how we experience the world outside of us. This filter can and will transform in our lifetime, and the question then will be if we are choosing how we want our filter to work and if it is for our betterment.

In the South we move to the element of fire and take this newfound connection to our body, the newly developed filter, that will allow us to see our truest self and put into motion how we choose to act and create this life. It brings a distinct reminder from our soul that we came here for a reason, and the element of fire will rekindle this reason.

Then we move **into the West** and into the depth of our emotional waters to clear what doesn't fit our journey on this spiral path. We'll explore why we feel what we feel after igniting our fire and use water to remove any last little bits that stop our soul from free, full delight.

The freedom we are seeking, which *can* be found, is sacred and it's magical.

We'll stay here in the North for the rest of this book to anchor in how the physical and spiritual properties of the earth and our body are the fundamental steps to get to our freedom.

We also have to look at the spiritual and energetic connections we hold onto that feed those old rotten apples inside us. These are called cords, energetic cords. We establish an energetic cord to every human (and living being on our planet), and those cords are attached to our body. Some are small and insignificant cords, such as the type you create when talking to a cashier at a store. Small ones are like energy the size of a piece of thread. Some are bigger, like the ones with our family, friends, and lovers. These are thick like big pieces of rope.

The cords are made of energy and exist in the nonmaterial worlds. As we know, our body holds the energy of every experience we've ever had. When these connections are old and stagnant, and often painful, we can remove them in an ancient and powerful ceremony called cord cutting. The ceremony begins with a series of rituals to put the practitioner into an altered state to cross time and space and see the energetic cords of another's body. It's possible to see the energy as a physical string that goes all around and into a body, and using a ritual knife, to cut that cord. A cord cutting is a ceremony that is done with smoke, sometimes with dancing, foot stomping, or modalities such as reiki.

The type of cord cutting I do includes a ritual knife, with which I go into the person's field, both spiritually and physically, and remove the connection that is causing the harm. It's powerful work, not the type of ritual that is light and easy for me or for the person receiving the cord cutting.

Of all the cord cuttings I've done, in at least seventy-five percent of them, I come across the most significant decaying and unhealthy cord in the pelvic area. It appears to me like a black hole that leaks black fog, negatively charged energy. The moment I detect this, I know this signifies sexual trauma. This may be hard to read, but you only need to do a quick online search to find out the number of women in our Western world that have some type of sexual trauma. Men do too, and these numbers are higher than you would imagine. Expanding that search to the rest of the world will curdle your belly when you realize how prevalent this is today. Experts estimate sexual trauma exists in more than eighty percent of women and in more than forty percent of men. And I can tell you that in my personal work with others, it is much higher.

In one such case, a family had asked me to do an energy clearing in their home. Energy clearings are a ritual that takes all the energy in a physical space and brings it to neutral in order to fill it with the desired energy.

Your Body Is the North

The family had four beautiful young children and a spacious home, yet they could feel heavy, dense energy. I entered their home and began to explain the process of using smoke and chanting to reset a physical space.

For this house clearing, I had a cauldron that held a lit charcoal, and I wore a sachet of mugwort, rose, and cedar around my neck.

Using chanting and a sacred smoke blend, I worked from the bottom of the house up, starting in the East, and cleansed each cupboard, closet, room, drawer, and space. I was looking for any dark, dense energy I could find to clear it and bring it to neutral. While I cleared the space, the family walked alongside me. We chanted together that we were removing all negative energy and were allowing in only love, family bonding, and joy. From bottom up through the full expansive house, and although I moved energy out of spaces that weren't used often, there wasn't anything heavy to clear, despite what the family had felt.

This is standard when I conduct energy clearing in homes for others in my practice as a witch. In more advanced cases, such as when people feel they have an entity or unwanted ghost, I start here then add more protective measures if needed.

In most cases it is not an outside entity that is creating the negative charge people feel when they call me for a house clearing. Most often, the negative energy comes from one member of the household or from old, stuck, dusty energy in physical parts of a home that haven't been used so the energy is stale.

This case was one of energy from one of the dwellers in the home. They weren't doing it on purpose; it was old trauma that was leaking from their body like a dense, dark cloud. Not only was it not done on purpose, but they also were unaware this was happening.

About halfway through clearing the house, I felt the pull from the mother. Her body became a little tighter, and her aura (the coloring around her body) was wavering. I witnessed it and continued to do the clearing while keeping this insight to myself. I had an immediate hit inside my own body (how I often see another's pain is by letting myself feel it inside me, temporarily, as a way to decipher what is happening). We finished the process that took us through their whole home, and the kids loved being a part of it.

I then asked if the kids could go play in another room, and I sat down and talked with the parents. I asked if I could do a clearing on the mom's body. Although they didn't know why, they agreed to allow me to clear her personal energy field. I knew she needed a cord cutting, but because I operate entirely on the principle of consent, and she had not asked for this, I focused on just an energy clearing with my smoke blend. I began the process by asking permission to use the smoke blend then chanting, using everything I had inside my own body and energy field to move what was stagnant.

She stood in the middle of the dining room, and I began an ancient chant, which is not in English, to call in the council of wise guides I walk with. Her arms were out to her sides and her eyes were closed, and I started circling her body with my smoke blend. I started near the back of her head and began walking around her, chanting and blowing the smoke toward her body. She began to tremble when I got close to her left hip around the back, and I could feel what was happening. I paused right there and held the smoke near her hip and the side of her womb. I was slowly and quietly chanting, whispering to the dark places inside her, moving the energy and transmuting it with the power of smoke in my hands. I knew she felt what was happening, as she began to cry and shake. I held the incense closer and increased my voice. I was entering the space closer and closer to her womb and had hit the energy field that held trauma.

I had slowly shifted my own state of energy, knowing we were entering the shadows inside her that were still stored in the place where physical trauma had taken place. I continued to combat the darkness and worked around her entire midsection down to the space between her legs. Round and round I moved with the smoke blend, getting louder and louder with my chant. She held her arms out the entire time and let the energy move. Then there was a shift in the field, and I could feel her understanding what was happening. She knew what

Your Body Is the North

I was feeling and what was moving out of her. She knew the trauma, and her mind began to process what was happening inside her body. As the energy continued to move out of her, the shaking stopped, and she surrendered and allowed the energy to be completely moved.

My psychic gifts showed me what I was clearing. She knew what I was clearing because her mind had allowed her to remember a painful experience she had buried in her shadows. But her husband did not know of this trauma. He stood to the side in disbelief at what was happening. He witnessed his wife shake and cry and heard my voice and could feel something big was happening. I moved the energy of the trauma out through the bottoms of her feet and the palms of her hands. I instantly realized that this was the source of what I had come for even if the family didn't know it. I did this with gentle hand movements that would appear from the outside as if I was moving air around her arms and legs.

When we began to slow the ritual, she slowly returned to her center and eventually opened her eyes and lowered her arms. I stood in front of her, and we gazed into each other's eyes, mine holding hers in a deep knowing that this beautiful, gentle woman carried very painful trauma. She said thank you and that she had forgotten about how much it still hurt inside of her.

We sat down and I explained there had not been any negative energy in the house and told them the house was clear and very open to this growing family's love and joy. I didn't explain the reason behind the mom's trauma; that was up to her to share if she so chose to, but I did explain that we had healed old wounds that likely caused any negative energy they had felt in the house.

I finished up quickly, as I knew the conversations that were to take place were private between the two of them. We had moved the trauma out of her body temporarily, but without therapy to address it, it would likely return. I didn't explain that this wound was now open and raw and would return when they had any type of intimacy with her body, as the trauma was still stored there. The wound would unknowingly release dark fields of energy. Each time her body was activated, that wound would be like a scab that was removed and would bleed dark energy into their home.

I'm sharing this part with you to illustrate the intensity of what the body can hold; I didn't share it with them at the time. I know the mom entered therapy shortly after and was working to heal the emotional trauma we had unearthed inside her body.

I'll pause here and offer a healing prayer to anyone reading this who knows exactly how she felt. Or if it's not you, look around your circle of friends and family and know this information is very important. More than half of everyone you know carries sexual trauma inside their bodies. Close your eyes and pray words of healing with me.

Great Mother Earth, we ask you to surround with your loving and gentle embrace the bodies of all humans that have suffered trauma in their bodies. Hold them. Show them how to reconnect to their wounds to heal them and close up any energy leaks that exist in those areas. Show them how loved they are and through the bounty of your nature's delight, help them return to a reconnection of themselves through your eyes.

I'll remind you that I am a witch. A powerful creator of shifts in the reality of people's lives. And you can be sure that if anyone I work on carries sexual trauma from another human, I most certainly also do a ritual, quietly and by myself, sending the perpetrators into a portal of their own making. Make no mistake about this being a part of my practice.

I wrote this chapter in several different ways, partially nervous about teaching people how to connect to their bodies when I know trauma has kept them disconnected. This isn't a traditional book that shies away from the raw and natural path of magic and real human life. Yet I know this will stop some readers, as they may prefer I speak only to the surface level of why so many people are not connected to their bodies. If you truly want to learn what real sacred magic is and how to use it to create what we call heaven on earth, then you have to start with the connection to your body.

Witch work is seeing and speaking the truth where others avoid it—even if you're only saying it to yourself.

This book isn't about sexual trauma, but do know that the bodies of women not only carry their own trauma but also that of their mothers. When we do this work to heal and connect to our body, we provide an example to our children. We are also clearing the energetic trauma that is carried down from mother to child. Healing ourselves means healing for our children and our grandchildren. It's very worthy of our time and love.

Doing this work is when we visit the underworld (the place where the shadows live) where trauma, shame, and pain reside. Those parts of you that you put aside—the experiences, feelings, and memories you don't speak of and hope to forget—are still there, and we can find them in the underworld and inside our body. If we do not address them, they will reappear and find a way to block any true experience of magic. At this point of the journey, we must get deeply comfortable with our body, all parts of it.

Rituals and spells are powerful, and they work but only as deeply as we are willing to feel it inside our body. If you cannot connect to your body and feel all the parts of it, the outcome of your desired ritual or spell will remain at surface level. In practicality, without addressing the connection to your body, I would only be giving half the truth. If you or anyone you know has not addressed this trauma, hold space for them to find therapy and trauma-informed coaches and release it. You can still do the work in this book while healing your trauma. But you may need more than what I am offering here. Please get support if you need it.

Now we'll move on to studying how this powerful magic works, which starts here in the North when we begin to examine our body and its connection to the cycles of nature.

When we study the North, we always discover more, as it's a direct study of our own body. We do this work in the North because we want to experience more joy and more aliveness, and to feel free enough to dance and sing. We want to turn on our spiritual and psychic gifts and let them be a clear, full conduit between our body and our soul (that ball of light that remains inside of us). Freedom lies on the other side of deep connection with our body.

Memory alone can show us where those scars live, as happened during the time at the cabin when I was time weaving and old wounds resurfaced in my body and those seeds became the greatest fertile ground for growing vines and flowers. We can heal the emotional and spiritual pain, and yet our body will always carry the sacred scars of time if we do not reacquaint ourselves with our own house, the flesh, cells, and bones that make up the complete package of humanness.

Even more so, everything we consume daily gets mixed up with unprocessed feelings and emotions trapped in our body. Overprocessed food, grease, and toxic substances are all contributing to keeping these parts of your body unhealthy. It is the same with toxic digital consumption, such as the news and the onslaught of ad rolls that algorithms feed you. The constant onslaught of negativity will take you so far away from your body that you'll become addicted to that faraway place that exists on the internet and isn't real. We stop that here and now when we go into our body, our connection to nature, and free ourselves of anything toxic. Keep in mind that you do not need to change your diet tomorrow and cut out every single thing you enjoy, but instead, become mindful of what you consume as a whole.

It's helpful while you are here in the North focusing on your own roots to notice how you're spending your time and give it a percentage. For example, see how much of your free time you spend scrolling versus how much you spend with yourself in nature. Look also at what you read. Is at least half of it joyful, fun, or funny? And does it make your belly hurt from laughing? Do the same with food—how much of what you consume is feeding your body nutrients versus how much is toxic. These are easy places to start and track with a percentage. Then begin to work that percentage to ensure the healthy consumption is greater than fifty percent for each area.

Your Body Is the North

A simple ritual to do this is a seven-day time-tracking exercise. Take out your journal and follow these steps.

1. Calculate how many free hours you have outside of work or other obligations and when you are not sleeping and create a total number of hours of free time you have in one single week.
2. Of that total of free time, track where the time is spent in thirty-minute increments. Do this daily so it is fresh in your mind. For example, when you wake up in the morning before you go to work, how did you spend that time? Family, food and coffee, getting ready for the day? How about right after work? Did you travel home, make stops, go to events, have family time, or crash on the couch? How many hours do you spend cleaning or shopping? What about family or friends? Whatever it is, track it in your journal for the seven days.
3. Make sure to include time spent scrolling social media, reading online publications, reading a book, listening to a podcast, etc. Track it all and write it down in your journal.
4. In the week you are tracking, also include time you spent exercising, going for a walk, meditating, casting spells, or doing rituals.

It might look something like this:

* Out of 168 hours per week available to us, approximately 55 are spent sleeping, and 40 to 50 of those hours are spent working.
* That leaves 73 hours of time while not sleeping and not working. Subtract 10 hours for day-to-day life such as cleaning, shopping, and cooking.
* If we roughly say that we have 60 free hours a week, how are we spending that time?

Then create a final conclusive list to see if at least fifty percent of that free time is spent doing things you love to do—time with people who bring you joy and happiness, being in nature, tending to your body and spirit. This is a very powerful ritual to do, as most of us have no idea how much time we lose by not paying attention to how precious our time is and using it with reverence and intention.

Everything we consume has an impact on our body. If we are not comfortable inside our skin or with our current state of feelings inside our body, then finding joy and exploring our definition of living a magical life will fall short of the goal of heaven on earth. It will feel like a lost, forgotten dream that lives only when your eyes are closed and cannot be reached in waking hours. I don't want that for you, for me, or for any of us.

We'll find the meaning of magic when our body feels good. You know those moments where you gasp in delight, bringing your hands to your heart and smiling so big that your face stretches? Those are the ways our body says yesss, thank you, more please.

Whatever you were doing that created that reaction, do more of that. When a deep breath outside stops you in your tracks, the smell of nature floods your entire system, and you feel a sense of calm overtake you, do more of that. Begin now and choose to do more of the day-to-day things that balance the busy and stressful parts of your life with the joyful and peaceful parts.

Although you may not be attuned to it, your body carries the history of your life's entire experience, both emotional and physical. This is why so many people walk around completely disconnected from the most sacred part of themselves—their body.

We prefer to look at other people's bodies on social media than look in the mirror. We see others' beauty and reflect on where we fall short, completely ignoring the miracle that we even wake up for another day.

Of course, our current capitalistic climate works hard to make us feel less than perfect, so we'll buy more stuff that we don't need.

Your Body Is the North

    This is why I'm here begging and preaching at you from the perch of a branch of a tree outside your window, beckoning you to come outside and play in nature and to feel it in your body. To be free to romp and roam, explore and expand.

    I once saw an ad in a city square of a thin model with the "right" hair and clothes that would fit only a young girl, and then I stopped and looked around. Of the hundreds of people around me, not one of them looked at all like her. They looked like beautiful human creations of different shapes and hair colors and were all so beautifully unique (even in their hustle of rushing by me). I stood there in that spot knowing that if any of them looked up at that sign and deemed it the "right" way to look, they would fall short. This is the way to make you want to buy more, change yourself, and be something different, the way to make you want what that brand is selling you—creating a false dream of their version of beautiful. It's all a complete hoax and is false and not born of reality; it's created to make you buy more, not grow and see the beauty in yourself.

    I can promise you that when you are in your final days, heading toward the death of your body, you will not be thinking about how much better the neighbor looked or how much prettier the picture your friend posted on Instagram was. You'll be questioning why you didn't pursue that dream you always had, didn't love harder, and didn't fulfill your soul's purpose.

    In my twenties, I met a very wise woman one day who told me she was a breast cancer survivor. I asked a lot of questions about how she made it through, and she said that when she got sick, she knew that deep inside her were many years of unprocessed trauma. Although she had treatment for the cancer, she didn't believe that's what cured her. She believed that she was cancer-free because she embarked on working out of her body the trauma she had carried for many years. She said that healing the trauma is what healed her body.

    I've never forgotten this powerful lesson. No amount of looking at just the surface of what may ail you will be enough. You have to go deeper into your emotional and spiritual connection to truly heal what needs to be healed. That's witch work. That's the work required to understand and actually feel magic, the spiritual realm, how your psychic gifts work, and the soul-level calling that brought you here in the first place.

When you have a gut feeling or your intuition comes online—it's inside your body.

When I say I use my seer vision, which is my primary psychic gift, it's happening inside my body in my mind's eye.

When you have an empathic feeling, it occurs inside of you at the core of your body, such as the belly, heart, and back.

Your spiritual gifts and the magic you can use to create new ways of living are explored and developed; you will find they are all inside of you. Your spiritual self, your soul, is housed inside of the holy, sacred temple known as your body.

Our body is the holiest of all, and it is holy because it carries all the parts of our soul, even if just for one temporary lifetime. And we know our body is temporary. We never know when our time is up. If we spend more time contemplating our death, we'll spend more time seeking joy. One of the final steps in experiencing sacred magic in this book will be to write your own obituary, not to be morbid but to bring you to this moment and the next moment and to live fully expressed in the short time you have here. And to remember that time in this body is fleeting and to spend more of it on what lights you up.

Life in the body encompasses a diverse range of experiences, some more desirable than others. Viewing life from the perspective of the body, you may recall moments of gratitude for your unique coloring, size, hair, and eye color, as well as times when you wished for different ones—moments of loving touch and moments of less loving touch, moments of solitude and moments of deep connection, and moments of pain and pleasure. You've had instances of physical strength and accomplishment alongside moments of weakness and vulnerability. Some may excel at honoring the physical body's limitations at various life stages, but there also might be times when one pushes too hard

Your Body Is the North

or buries the pain too deeply and faces the consequences. You carry all of that around with you every moment of the day, like a hard drive of memories stored in your cells. It becomes the lens through which you view yourself and the world around you at any given time. Questing for magic seeks to level the playing field so you see yourself through the lens of your soul, not the lens of a clothing model on the internet.

When you set yourself free from these constraints and touch and move your own body to the rhythm of joy and happiness, not giving two fucks what anyone thinks, you have entered the zone of true sovereignty. That's sacred magic.

In addition to bodily experiences, many beliefs have been ingrained in religious traditions that perpetuate a false division between the spiritual and material realms, leaving you lost with how to be connected to your body and also connected to "god."

> *I say that our body is a reflection of all things considered god.*
> *Our beauty, our wrinkles, our imperfections—it's all divine.*

While in the bathtub as part of my healing ritual in the story I shared, a new definition of beauty took root in my soul, and I have since viewed my body, other bodies, and our earth all as expressions of beauty. Where our scars reside, our beauty grows. Where our connection to our body increases, all connections to others and nature can be seen and felt.

When we walk the path of the North, we see that our body is connected to nature, and nature is connected to our body. There's no room in connecting to nature if you carry around a judgment because your body doesn't look a certain way. Have you ever entered a forest and picked out the prettiest trees and told the rest they are ugly? No, they are just different, and we accept that universal truth yet find it so painful to accept the same of ourselves.

We must connect and reconnect to our body if we are to find any type of feeling that we would identify as magical. Slowly. Gently. With care, in order to understand where we might be out of balance. Moving into your body is the greatest resource you have to access your spiritual gifts. It is sacred work to make our physical flesh feel joy, such as taking a bite of chocolate, having orgasms, freely dancing in the rain, or stomping your feet in ritual.

Pause reading this book for a moment and let's find something that will bring your body joy in this exact moment. For example, stand up and move and shake your body, roll your hips in a circle, stretch your arms over your head, and breathe deep into your belly and let it out with a sigh. Once you've done this, put on a favorite song and dance or lie flat on the ground outside, and feel the feelings that come up in your body. Aah, it feels so good to actually move and feel our body.

I have much more for you in Part Two that will help you begin the process of connecting to the place that holds your life experiences, caring for them and healing them. And reconnecting to the greatest resource you have available to you in this lifetime—your perfectly created flesh and bone. It's a place where your heart beats to keep you alive without you even having to ask and where your cells heal because you regenerate them with your thoughts and mindset.

Your body is alive and lives as one organism whose single purpose is to provide your soul with housing. This means it listens to your voice and your thoughts—giving power to your mind to tell it what to do.

Sit with that for a moment and take it in. Do you ever wonder why that when you worry about getting sick, you do? Or do you notice how, if are afraid you'll fall doing a certain activity so you don't do it, you fall the next day over a crack in the sidewalk? Your body was listening to your brain and obeying.

Start telling your body what you really want to experience. Speak it aloud several times a day:

Body, I want to move the energy that feels stuck and isn't helping my soul.

Body, I want to feel you more deeply to feel more joy.

Your Body Is the North

Body, I want to connect with you and learn to love you.

Body, I want my psychic gifts turned on so I can hear my soul.

Thank you, body. I am you and you are me and we are one.

Speak words of joy, fun, pleasure, connection, and psychic insights. Turn your body into the workhorse that it is, working for you to have and be what you want. Now is the perfect time to begin!

Doing the work to reconnect to your body will awaken your senses so deeply that you'll wonder how you lived so long being disconnected. You'll learn to love the smell of a fresh peach on a summer day, and when you smell it then taste it, it will become an entire ritual in itself that you feel deep in your body.

I witness many spiritual practitioners and witches who focus on teaching "out-of-body" experiences and astral travel, which has their place. We'll cover this in book two in the direction of the East and the element of air, but if we cannot return to our body and bring it into our human experience, we're missing the point. That's why we are here on the first step of sacred magic, because our body is the key to it all.

While reading this, take time in the North to explore the areas of connection and disconnection from your body. If you carry unprocessed trauma, you'll find it in the body. I invite you to take it slow and take your scars and let flowers bloom in their place. Let yourself reconnect with your greatest resource in this lifetime, your body.

You'll find rituals and practices to reconnect to your body in Part Two. Choose one and do it for thirty days. You'll see major changes in how your spiritual and psychic gifts change when you connect with the senses of your body.

Contemplation questions

1. If I'm completely truthful with myself, how do I feel about my body? Why?

2. I've disconnected from my body because …?

3. Where do I feel joy in my body?

4. Where do I carry tension?

5. What am I willing to do to create a deeper connection to my body?

Chapter Six
Winter

As we connect deeper into our body on this journey, it can have moments of heaviness in understanding how we got to whatever level of connection or disconnection we currently have. Another way to frame it in your mind so you can see and feel the significance is by thinking of it as a time for calibration to our own truth about our lives so far. By calibration, I mean bringing ourselves to neutral and knowing where we are in or out of alignment.

If we want to make our lives better, more fulfilling, and definitely more magical, think of this step on the journey as a time to rest. Resting and recalibration are what we do every night when we sleep. Resting and recalibration are part of the cycle of life in all things, as we've learned with plants, trees, and nature, and with our body.

Keep in the forefront of your heart that this is merely a stop along the way of this path of magic. It's not the destination nor a place we plan to be in for long. It's a time to sit, explore, move, and then move forward along the spiral.

Another facet of understanding the North is understanding what season it represents.

Our planet passes into and through seasons continually, without fail, every year of all the years it's been here. History tells us there have been colder years, warmer years, and everything in between. Science tells us that the seasons change based on where we live and how close where we live is to the sun at any point and time.

We'll bring the sun closer on our path the closer we get to the second step of the spiral path of magic when we move from the North and into the East.

The North is the winter and the long nights of the darkest season where our body craves more rest and a slower pace. The winter is the hours after dark in the twenty-four hours that we count as our days.

The East is the spring and the early morning hours when we rise from slumber.

The South is the summer and the peak of the hot season and is found in the middle of our days.

The West is the fall when seasons change and we begin to plan for the upcoming winter. The West is where we wind down our days and move into the evenings.

Since we are in the North, let's explore what it feels like to be in the winter season of your soul and spiritual path.

Winter

I recently took myself to the North to honor my desire for a great rest. The great rest became a sacred pause. When we take a sacred pause, we are stepping into the winter that is found in the North.

Leading up to this calling for a pause, I had launched a new YouTube channel, experienced massive growth on social media, and increased my client base for both businesses I run. I had become very busy. My nonspiritual business (international nonprofit leadership) was and is something I'm still passionate about, and I do much work in the nonprofit field.

The Spellbinders Club had been born as part of my mystery school, the content I was creating was generating massive interest, and I led hundreds of others across the veil (leaving the human realm and moving into the spiritual realm) every week in the school.

In the middle of this expansive time, my mother's health had begun to decline. Dementia was worsening, and plans for her to be transferred to long-term care needed to be put in place. My family was, and still is, grieving from transitioning my mother to assisted living. When the process began, my mom was confused and was refusing to move.

Since my mother and her side of the family live a long distance from me, it was time for me to visit and assist with the plans. This led to a series of flights, car rentals, and all the emotions that come with our parents' declining health.

On the first trip to see my mother while she was still in her home, I contracted food poisoning and ended up spending a night in the hospital.

On the second trip to see her after she had a fall and was admitted into the hospital, I contracted the virus that many of us still don't want to speak of and was sick the entire trip.

On the third trip the weather was frigid cold, and my family was at odds over emptying her home. The relationships with my family mirrored the frigid weather.

The increase in business growth and media exposure and changing family dynamics all happened within three months. This was also happening as I turned fifty and had plans to travel to a warm, beautiful island in the Caribbean to celebrate.

I was recording content from my mother's living room couch by candlelight. I was moonlighting my daily workload and daylighting as a daughter to a mother going through the final stages of her life in her home and in the hospital.

I took twelve flights during this time, for my mother, for my birthday, and to see family over the holidays. I launched new programs while at home, crafted spells, crossed the veil, engaged in hour upon hour of business management. I was treading water and couldn't keep my head above water for much longer. Just thinking of it causes me to lose my breath momentarily and hang my chin on my chest. It was exhausting.

My body was tired from the illnesses, and I could feel the heavy, dense energy both in my physical body and in my energy field. I worked hard daily to clear my energy and return to my center. But I was still tired and couldn't get my energy back to 100 percent. Like a cell phone, I had a low battery for weeks.

One day, I was on a call with one of my magical team members (staff), discussing the schedule, operating procedures in a mystery school, and the new schedule for YouTube content, when suddenly, my body screamed a great big NOPE.

It was a strong message to stop. Just stop. Before I knew what was happening, I said nope out loud and that I didn't want to do this.

I took a few deep breaths while on the call to let what had just happened sink in. I had just heard and listened to my body say "wait a minute." I had verbally spoken it aloud at the same time it had happened inside my body. I took a breath and returned to the conversation and explained what I was feeling. I needed a break, a pause to replenish my energy, and I wanted to stop everything. It was a full-stop scream inside me, and even after breathing through it, the feeling remained. I had made an instantaneous decision and stuck with it.

Winter

I emailed everyone on my team that I wanted to pause everything, with no date of when it would resume. No social media posts, no newsletters, nothing that would require me or my involvement. I'm a very advanced planner, so there was already a lot in motion and scheduled. Because of this, nobody outside my inner circle knew I had entered a great pause until I came out of it and shared in my community what had occurred. I went into complete disconnection, physically, mentally, and spiritually. I maintained what I had committed to in programs, classes, students, and nonprofit clients. Everything else that involved creating new content or new programs came to a standstill.

During the sacred pause, I also took a good hard look at the disharmony that had begun to swirl like a gray cloud in my extended family, and I decided to take a sacred pause from them, too, remaining only in touch with my mother and her partner.

I spent many weeks in this winter of my soul during this sacred pause. I spent time in solitude and let myself just be. I sat in a part of my home where I had a chair I called my thinking chair and rested. I journaled and processed what I was feeling and how my body was carrying what I was feeling. I began returning to rituals I use in times of big emotional processing. I stomped my feet and cried with the music turned up full blast. I spent hours outdoors in nature. I was walking and sitting in equal parts. I talked to the trees around my home and asked for comfort. I used plant allies to make healing teas and sacred smoke many times during the day to move and shift my feelings. I honored myself, knowing I was in the winter during the sacred pause.

In the evenings I danced by myself, more slowly, by candlelight with a soft fuzzy blanket around my shoulders. I moved to the beat of what I was feeling during this period. And I slept a lot.

I allowed myself to grieve the changing of my family and the changing of my heart. I allowed myself to release the big hits of dopamine that kept coming while my public platform was growing. I let it all go and went inward. I often felt like I was holding my own heart in my hands during this time and giving it love; I felt tender and, well, human. I still do since then and keep this tenderness close, as I know it holds the medicine my busy life often needs.

And then, at the end of the first month of this sacred pause, I felt colors and dreams return to my imagination. I started singing my favorite songs again with more energy and letting my feet move to the beats I liked. I began allowing myself to dream again of what I wanted to do, what I had done that I loved doing, and what I no longer wanted. I fertilized the soil of my intentions as we do in the winter. I let old branches (programs and schedules) die and decay. I let my body turn every facet of my life into winter vegetation in order to decide what I would foster and regrow and what I would let remain as compost.

I knew I needed to close many doors for new ones to open. I knew I would be moving along this spiral path and eventually choose to go back to the East and begin again. Ever so slowly, I allowed a little speed to return then paused again to ask, "Was I ready?" or "Was this what would make me happy?" I moved slowly when I wanted to speed up again. I paused again when I wanted to move quickly, continually coming back to my body to see how it felt. I realized I didn't enjoy much of what I had launched and was still doing it only because I thought I needed to. I also realized how much I love my nonprofit work and wanted to continue fostering that side of my business.

I continued to move out of the winter phase of my life and turned my vision, my heart, and my mind to the East to prepare for what would be left after this sacred pause. I permanently canceled many free and ongoing classes I had been offering. I resigned from volunteer roles I held with nonprofit organizations, and I removed myself from courses I was a student in but never had the time to attend, unsubscribed to hundreds of email lists, and cleared anything off my schedule that didn't feel like a "fuck yes" in my body. I permanently canceled several of the posted schedules I had in the Facebook groups I held. I said goodbye to relationships that weren't equally loving exchanges but had become one way, where others desired my magic and bright light but weren't returning it. I reduced my own playing field down to the basics. I went back to focusing on what felt good in my body, and everything else became the sacred no.

None of this was in my awareness during the months before the sacred pause happened, when I was busy running and growing my businesses while also grieving. Instead, I was on cruise control, allowing more and more into my field. I kept saying yes. I said yes to one expert who told me how to run marketing, I said yes to one who told me what I needed to do in my Facebook groups, and I said yes when my team told me I needed to add a new offering. I just kept saying yes. I didn't realize this had happened until I entered the sacred pause and gained clarity by asking myself—"What am I doing?" That's what time spent in the North does. That's why it's the spiritual winter season. I had to start saying no in order to find alignment. Saying no is what happens in the sacred pause.

For the first time in many years, I wanted less of everything and to have more of me for me. I stopped giving to others to provide more to myself. My own magic had been weeping inside, and in my busyness, I ignored it to keep up, to grow, to post more, to reach more people, and to listen to the experts tell me what I needed.

I have done this work for years and teach others to do the same. Yet I had found myself overgiving to the point of depletion. It happened slowly over time, a little more here, a yes to that, a little more there, and I found myself overcommitted and underloved by myself. I needed to swallow my own medicine and return to the basics of what I teach to replenish and recharge myself.

What happened after I was ready to come out of this pause is mind-blowing, even to me. One thing was returning to writing this book. I have created this outline about twenty times. I have written parts over and over for years. I wanted to do this, but I didn't have the space.

I continued to emerge from the winter and slowly allowed things and people back that aligned with this new version of myself that was slowly beginning to grow out of the compost I had turned my life into. I chose to leave the rest on pause, not bringing it back into my field at this time and instead fostering it like fertilizer for what was coming next. I embraced the sacred no many times to say yes to more of what aligned for me. I knew what the yeses were by how my body felt. I followed the yeses, and if I felt a no, I said no. It felt like a dose of fresh, cool oxygen in my lungs to move into the winter and rest for a while. To take the pressure off all the ways I had allowed myself to become beholden to others.

The winter is the North because it's a time similar to when the earth slows down its growing season and turns its attention to fostering the roots of what's going to grow next. When you allow yourself to see the winter season of your soul as a time to recharge your own roots (energy), you find more clarity in what you want to create next.

It's important when you are in the winter season of your life to continue to come back to your body and ask yourself, "Is this what I want, will this create the future I want, and is this nourishing and watering my own seeds?" When you stay connected to your body in this process, it will give you great insight.

Let's pause a moment here and practice what a no and a yes feel like in your body. I'll provide more details in the rituals section of this book, but we can do it easily here with a few simple steps:

1. Start by placing your right hand on your heart and your left hand low on your belly.
2. Take five deep belly breaths, with ten counts in and ten counts out.
3. Prime the yes by saying aloud "Is my name (and say your name)?" You'll get a feeling inside, then say out loud, "This is what a yes feels like."
4. Repeat this question for four things you know about yourself, each time saying, "This is what a yes feels like."
5. Then take five more deep breaths and keeping your hands where they are, ask a question that you know the answer is no, such as the wrong

age, the wrong place you live, or any other incorrect statement about yourself.
6. When your body feels the no inside, say, "This is what a no feels like."
7. Do this four times.
8. Shake your hands and arms afterward to release the ritual.

You can come back to this practice to keep priming your body to give you fast, quick yeses and nos. The more you practice this, the easier and faster you will learn what the two different feelings are. Then the next time you want to make a decision, come to your body and ask it a yes or no question and trust the answer.

The North is the season of winter, where the earth is encompassed in the dark, and the wind whispers ancient secrets that say to rest. The barren branches that appear to have stopped living are a sacred place of stillness in the silent nights. The birds have flown to new homes, and our body craves time for introspection. It's a season of choosing ourselves over what others want from us. Remembering that it is a choice is part of the spiral path of magic and helps us choose more aligned actions as we go along.

As we quest for a deeper, more enchanted and fulfilling way of life, we look inward in the season of winter. It is the place where we find the deepest sacred magic and gather around a fire with our soul for warmth to tell stories to ourselves and honor the wisdom in the cycles of everything we are experiencing, with the goal of coming out of the time wiser and more connected.

The seasons impact the earth as they do our body. Regardless of where you live, even if there is one season year-round, the earth changes due to its proximity to the sun. When the distance from the sun changes, the earth creates changes. When the earth changes, so does our body.

Our body goes through seasons, too, which are not always the same as the weather changes. When we study the North and how it resonates at our soul level, we look at the properties of winter and can determine if our body is in a winter phase. The soul has seasons, from dark nights to explosive radiance, from stormy and destructive endings to new beginnings. This is also how Mother Nature brings her seasons inside of us because we are all connected.

The winter (North) is the time our mind, body, and soul need rest and reflection to provide nourishment to the roots of our lives.

The spring (East) is the time we choose what seeds we want to plant and gently place them into our goal list to be rooted and nurtured.

The summer (South) is the time we see the seeds turn into plants, and our plans move along, and we grow and move.

The fall (West) is when we harvest all we have created, and we relish in the new growth and take it all inside to prepare to start the cycle all over again.

We can also choose to move from anyplace on the great elemental wheel and take ourselves into a season that we need and pause there for a while. This could be in just one area of our life like careers or relationships. As I did in the story I shared of the sacred pause, I chose to put myself in a time-out and went intentionally into the winter season to rest and evaluate my life. It wasn't that I was disconnected from my body or in the underworld; it was me trapped in the season of summer with too much fire and everything was burning, even my heart. Before the sacred pause, I would have considered myself to be in the South—passion, action, and motivation, saying yes to any and all opportunities to grow and travel. When I said "nope," I immediately moved into the North. I didn't pass around the circle to get to the North and hang in the East or West. I immediately passed go and plopped myself into the sacred pause and into the winter.

Winter

Seasons of the soul are powerful ways to work your growth and magic. Once you can identify what season you are in, you can feed your soul with what it needs in that season, and you can also count on the fact that the season will change. Each stop in any season of our soul and our life will change and progress. Studying magic and the sacredness of transformation means choosing to take the steps, with intention and clarity about why you are there and what you can learn while there. It's all connected and it's all sacred magic.

The North brings rest and reflection to replenish our soil and tend to our roots.

The East is where we go when we need to redefine our beliefs and plant new seeds of ideas or intentions.

The South is where we put our intentions into action and fuel the fire behind them.

The West is where we go to water the growth and harvest what we have created.

These soul-season cycles can happen within a single week or month or sometimes take place throughout the year. Let's feel the stillness and crisp air as we venture to this place in hushed tones, accepting the invitation to step deeper inward, as I did during the sacred pause.

We've looked at the earth through a fresh lens, our connection to plants, and how it's all reflected in our body. Now we look at the part of the North that represents the beauty and simplicity of the quiet. The replenishment of our soil and the roots of each aspect of our lives.

Take a moment to make a list of everything you have going on in your life, and underneath each area of your life, ask yourself the following.

Am I resting in this area, such as in my job or business or perhaps a relationship that's gone stale, and not sure what's next? Write winter if the answer is yes.

Is this something that feels stale or isn't growing and I would like to explore letting it go? Write winter if the answer is yes.

Then give yourself some space to write out your intention to allow the winter to be the time to bring clarity into each of these areas and use the yes/no ritual to ask yourself what's next.

Think of the North as a winter landscape where the trees are barren and quiet, the branches turned to finger-like arrows pointing in all directions, reminding you that when you awaken again from this season, you can move in any direction you desire. The introspection and reflection time will till the soil you will use to plant the next seeds of growth. It's a time to find joy in the darkness. To feel the waning sun and see the beauty even when everything appears dead and frozen.

Not to be the bearer of bad news, but the truth is you must walk in winter many times in your life, often yearly and many times monthly, when we have brought too much heat (anger), too much air (disconnected from our path), or too much water (unmotivated) and need to regroup. You may walk in the North for a day or two or even a few weeks at a time. You will never know how long you will be in the North until you get there and begin to unravel what brought you there and keep unraveling until you are ready to move on into the East.

It's the sacred pause, the time to care for our body and create deeper connections to ourselves and give less to the outside world. All our time in the North is this, but when we look through the eyes of winter, we can understand the feelings of the North. It's the time of a private party for one, where what you want and what you need are all you focus on.

Winter

It does not matter what the physical weather is outside. You are in the winter spiritually when you are called to evaluate your feelings of belonging or lack of belonging or when you feel like you've lost stability and crave safety from life's chaotic energy. We can choose to step into winter in the North just by allowing ourselves the sacred pause of it all.

Winter is also the time when we face our shadows. This is a central role of growth, going deep into our subconscious mind or the underworld as a way to sit in our soil and remove anything that will hinder the seeds we desire to plant. When I entered the sacred pause that I shared with you, it was also a deep revealing of my shadows. My shadows contain old beliefs about how important it is for me to overdeliver, to give because I can. I hold a shadow belief that I must be there when someone asks, regardless of how deeply it depletes me. The time I spent in that sacred pause was to process and acknowledge the shadow that I continue to work through all the days of this human life.

In these deep times of winter, we are called to shine a light on the darkest corners of our soul and learn to embrace the shadows, the parts of us we keep hidden out of fear of judgment, shame, and anxiety.

I took myself to the North when I realized I was trying to make my family, staff, and students happy with what they needed from me. I was overdelivering what I thought people needed. I was mostly scared of letting people down. It turns out it was me that I let down, and I was burning too hot and too fast. I was plowing through what needed to be done, even with my witch work, focused on the next thing on my to-do list. It crept up on me like a slow-burning fire until it consumed me. I went to the North to roll around in the winter of my soul to put the blaze out.

We can only explore this if we are willing to slow down. We need to move softer and more tenderly into confronting our deepest fears and insecurities to unravel the conditioning that has led our lives up to this point. How often have you distracted yourself from what you don't want to think about by scrolling social media? Or maybe your form of distraction comes in the form of a drink at night to escape all the stressors of the day. We all have ways in which we avoid the truth and keep pushing forward on our list of shoulds and have tos.

One of the most common ways I see people avoid confronting their feelings is by staying overly busy, by keeping a jam-packed schedule at work and filling all their spare time with activities, time with friends and family, shopping, events, and on it goes.

In my spiritual coaching work, when I work with people one-on-one, this is one of the first questions I ask: "What is your typical schedule like?" When I ask when they make time for stillness or time by themselves in nature, they pause and usually say something like, "But I have to work, I'm busy, my kids need me, my family wants me, or I have to do these things." When we go through and delete these shoulds and have tos, it becomes easy to see that there is always time in our schedule for stillness. To make time for it means putting yourself at the top of your priority list.

This idea might bump up against your own beliefs about what makes a good person, a good parent, a good employee, or a good family member. We've been conditioned to be the "good" person by giving to others. What strange creatures we are that we carry the beliefs that we should give more of ourselves than we even possess to be a "good" human. It isn't entirely true that you can't pour from an empty cup; you can. What you pour from your cup when it's empty, however, is just hollow nothingness, which isn't the best you doing the pouring. Or you may bump up against your beliefs about the material things you need to be happy, which keeps you on the hamster wheel of busyness. Are you still looking for the things outside of you to make you happy? The right job or car? Have you been sacrificing the needs of your soul for material gains? This is what we look at when we are in the North.

Do an evaluation now of how much you are giving to others versus giving to yourself. This is best done when you take time for yourself to practice deep breathing and journal. Here are a few prompts to start with.

- How many hours of my waking days am I rushing?
- What events or activities do I do because others want me to, but if I'm honest with myself, I don't enjoy?
- Where am I wasting time distracting myself with another activity, scrolling social media, or doing things I don't love because I get bored just sitting still?
- Am I angry more often than not?
- In the last month, how many hours have I dedicated to taking care of just me and only me?

This will give you insight on where you need more rest, stillness, and a slower pace. If you find yourself in chaos and too busy to even complete the exercise, try this mantra in your mind and think it through slowly: *Slow is steady, and steady is smooth, and smooth becomes fast.*

When we move slowly, we become steady in our energy. When we are stable and steady in our energy, how we move day-to-day becomes smooth. When we move smoothly, we can then go about our life, goals, intentions, and creations in a much faster way. This is 100 percent true in every single area of your life. The winter means asking yourself how you can move more slowly, to become steady, which will lead to living smoothly then fast in a more intentional way.

Combining this "slowly forward" way of mind with time in nature is a true clearing of the path to happiness that you may have mistakenly thought existed outside of you. We must go to this place in the North to recharge and recenter. Living without taking time in the North on a daily basis of stillness is disconnecting from your soul's purpose. When taking time in stillness becomes part of your everyday life, you will be less likely to need a giant sacred pause and be less likely to burn out.

I get it. I really do understand why this happens over time. Our time gets crept into, and we get into the habit of filling our spare time with unhealthy activities like mindlessly scrolling social media or staying too busy. Fear of missing out sets in, and the next thing you know, there isn't an evening free on your schedule for an entire month. I get that to stop doing so and begin scheduling time to do nothing but sit with yourself can be uncomfortable. When you take time to sit with yourself, everything you've been avoiding thinking about bubbles to the surface.

Yet I'm here to tell you that this different way, this way to your truest happiness and magic, requires this of you. I will also tell you that you will return to this cycle often and need to realign. We all need time to process any occurrence in our life, whether it be an amazing experience with friends or a challenging one. We still need time to process our feelings, and we can process our feelings only when we are in stillness.

I deeply desire that you to take time in the winter regularly so you can find a few good deep breaths of yourself. A few moments for deep thinking each day so you are processing as you go. A few hours in nature to connect to the bigger picture and the cycles you are unknowingly perpetuating. Not doing this separates us from our magic and the power to create life on our terms; instead, it allows life to bump us through the path like a pinball.

To be in winter regularly means to be OK with being uncomfortable with yourself. See the dark, the stillness of the imaginary winter, and look inward. This is where we learn self-compassion, perspective, and perseverance. It's a practice to explore what's in our field and if we have been avoiding it.

If we resist, it's like trying to make it snow when it's a 90-degree day outside. That just isn't possible, no matter how skilled you are at spell casting. Violating the laws of nature does not work. The same applies to our body and our growth. If you're hiding from what you really need to think and feel, then you are likely calling more of that exact same experience into your life by not clearing it and grounding it into the lesson itself.

I understand why we do it and why it's easier to get a dopamine hit, or maybe even a hit of real dope like drugs or alcohol, but if you want to explore what real magic feels like, you'll find it on the other side of healing what lives in your shadows and taking time to think about what you really want in life and by discovering if your day-to-day reflects what you want. If you're going to truly find your path to feeling centered and connected to your purpose, joy, and contentment, time with yourself in the North is needed.

Start by making small changes to your schedule. Add fifteen minutes daily, then increase it to a few hours on the weekend. Sit in silence with yourself, even if that means going to a park nearby or anywhere outdoors.

Not all time spent in the North will be dedicated to exploring your shadows or processing big feelings; sometimes it's just for a rest. Or for the joy of it. You'll find yourself remembering there was a great book you've wanted to read. Or remember that you like to walk outdoors to your favorite tunes. Joy comes in the solitary time, but it takes time to get there.

Contemplation questions

1. When was the last time I had a full day or several days just to myself?

2. Explain the reasoning for the above answer.

3. Do I feel guilty at taking time for myself? What have I learned about that and where in life have I learned it?

4. Do I have a practice of being in nature or connecting to my body that I can add in? Why not?

5. What do I enjoy doing by myself that I do not feel I have enough time for?

6. Have I lost passion for what I love about my job, my family, or any part of my life?

Chapter Seven
Sacred Spaces of the North

The spaces we live and work in are alive with energy. Our homes, offices, and even vehicles contain and hold power. The energy of all physical spaces can either connect you to your intentions or work against what you want to feel if you do not put time and attention into creating them with thought and care. The size, location, or type of material doesn't matter—it's all energy. Wood, shingles, bricks, and metal are all vibrational energy fields.

Let me tell you about a time when my home, a space I intentionally created down to every last room as an extension of myself, communicated with me in a wild way, even by my standards as someone who teaches others how to create sacred spaces.

I felt strange and the air in my home was dense and heavy. I burned my favorite blend of clearing herbs and did a blessing in each corner of each room to no avail. And I felt so tired. For a week, I needed at least thirty minutes each afternoon to lie under a warm blanket on the couch. I couldn't shake the heaviness. Initially, I thought it must be the weather that was making me so tired. I tapped into my inner knowing fields a few times to gain insight, but no clear answers came through.

Something felt off, and I couldn't pinpoint it. I didn't understand what was happening, and I chalked it up to the busyness of upcoming travel, my long to-do list, and the chill in the air. I wanted to slow down and feel what was happening, but the hours and days were ticking by, and I needed to keep pushing through.

Then on a day when it was cold outside and the wind was blowing across the ocean, the walls of my house shuddered. I was preparing to leave on a trip when the strangeness began. Pictures on the wall began to hang unevenly. A vase fell from a shelf, splattering water and glass shards over the carpet, leaving my beautiful altar roses on the floor. When I bent down to pick them up, I misjudged the distance and cracked my head on a table edge. Ouch, it hurt. I pressed one of the roses from the floor to my head to give love to the ache. I muttered under my breath several times, "What is going on?"

I quickly circled all of my altars, cleaned the spaces, and refilled the water chalices to the West of each area of my home. I dusted and organized books and removed any remaining items that felt stale. I wanted the lightness back in my house before I left, so I performed all the house-clearing rituals. I had to do the rituals quickly, as the departure clock was ticktocking away.

And yet, things were still weird.

I brought a small black suitcase upstairs, unzipped it, and added sweaters and layers, as it was cold where I was going. As soon as I tried to add my boots to the pile, I realized the bag wouldn't close. I decided to go downstairs to get a larger bag for my trip and put the smaller one away. When my feet reached the second-to-last step into the downstairs area, it felt like there was no longer a stair. My foot floated for much longer than usual and then came crashing down. The bag flew out of my hands. *Where did the last stair go?* I looked, and it was still there, even though my foot had missed it. *Weird,* I thought. I reminded myself to slow down, even when my to-do list was looming.

I carried the bigger bag upstairs and began reloading my items. Just then, I looked down and saw a flash of movement under my bed. It wasn't so fast that I didn't notice what it was. Oh. Emm. Gee. It was a mouse. The mouse ran by and disappeared under my bed. I paused only for a moment and felt a little panicky then quickly refocused and resumed packing knowing I had only a few hours left until I needed to be in bed if I wanted any chance of sleep before my departure. I thought, *How bad can it be to have a mouse in my home for one night?* I decided to deal with it later and began my evening rituals for sleep.

I closed the zipper and walked to the edge of my room with only a slight hesitation, wondering where my new little furry friend had gone, but I thought, *Nah, he's sleeping too.* I figured that mice and humans could coexist for one night.

I snuggled in and put my glasses on to read a new book I had just been gifted, excited to start something fresh as I drifted off for only a few hours of sleep. Having no idea what it was about, I opened the first chapter and began to read about a man experiencing the emotions of his home when he and his wife were about to have their first child. I was immediately hooked by his experience of connecting with his home's emotions and learning that his own emotions had been absorbed by his deep connection to his physical space. It was fascinating and weird to be reading about this as I had experienced many connections to my home in the past.

As I continued reading, I learned that the man's house welcomed their new baby, and he felt more and more emotions that took him weeks to realize weren't his own. His home was feeling its own feelings. I skipped ahead several chapters in the book because I had a buzzy feeling in my belly telling me this was important.

Sacred Magic

Later in the book, he explains that when the child was older and the family needed to move to a bigger space, the house started showing its sadness. Things began moving around in his space. Random items tilted slightly. Things fell off walls. The energy felt dense, and he was often tired from the home's energy. The book was explaining how this man realized that he was feeling the direct and powerful emotions that were coming from his house itself. He even fell off a ladder while taking down a picture to pack for his upcoming move.

His story was about learning how his home was expressing sadness that he was leaving. In that instant, I realized my home was expressing sadness that I was leaving too. Bingo, my body instantly became aware that my home had been speaking to me since I had booked my flight. I thought back to the weird energy of the last few days and all that had occurred, and it brought an electrical current through my veins when I realized what had been happening. I was feeling my house's sadness.

Then, in one crazy moment, as I tilted my book down to think, my new mouse friend, who must have made his way to a shelf to the left of my bed, catapulted off the shelf and landed on the floor past the end of my bed. My book light illuminated him as if it were his own personal stage light. I momentarily sat frozen in my bed trying to fathom what had just happened. Have you ever seen a mouse fly off a shelf, Superman-style, in front of you? Now things were really weird. I giggled a little and freaked out a lot.

I gave up the idea of sleeping and decided to focus on what was happening in my home. I went to the main area of my living room and sat in the darkness until my eyes adjusted. I took a deep breath and smelled the roses that had spilled earlier that day, their memory still leaving a faint trace of smell. I ran my fingers along the soft carpet and stilled my hands to feel the energy my home had been trying to express.

It was sad I was leaving, and it wanted me to stay and continue filling it with love and joy. It wanted me home and had been expressing its sadness through the material world—the items falling, me falling, heavy and sad energy, and, eventually, a pesky mouse to interrupt my packing.

I lit a candle and performed a sacred rite for my home, thanking it for loving me. I completed a visualization exercise that created a cord between my heart and the center of my space, almost like an umbilical cord. I lay down and let the cord connect deep into my heart, then into my belly, then expand throughout the house. That did it. The house immediately felt lighter as I reassured it that I would return soon.

I closed the ceremony and spoke aloud to my home, asking for no more mice and promising an offering upon my return.

There is a divine and deep connection between us and the spaces we dwell in. Although I've known and have been teaching this for many years, the concept had never been as straightforward as it was at that moment when I was preparing to leave. I was too busy to notice. I chalked up the moving pictures, the fall, and the mouse as random occurrences. I was too focused on departing to recognize how my leaving impacted my house and its energy.

You may not talk to your house or feel it shudder and wobble when you leave, but it can hold the energy you mindfully intend. Your home is connected to you very deeply, as you and it together become one big breathing energy field. The word "home" has many meanings and can be many things, both inside us and within physical spaces. Your physical home, or the dwelling you reside in, might be a small, shared space or a large, sprawling space. Yet the connection between you and your physical home will become one energy field. The question isn't whether or not that happens; it's whether or not you give your time and attention to create a connection that serves your needs. Your home can hold the feeling of safety to be yourself, dance wild and free, and slow down and rest. It's the place to express love, happiness, and connection—or at least, that's what's possible. Your home can also be the place you go to navigate big and hard emotions.

We can examine our homes by evaluating the cardinal directions within them. Feng shui is a powerful practice, and feng shui practitioners are witches of energy—my nickname for them. If feng shui interests you, it's worth researching and finding a practitioner to dive deeper into this area.

Sacred Magic

Your dwelling is alive with energy. It is pulsing, feeling, and creating alongside you. Your home is a sentient space that carries the life form of what you give it. You can clear your space, take it to neutral, then fill it with the energy you need at any moment. This process is neither complex nor complicated, and it doesn't require big ceremonial magic; it only requires you to take the time and give your spaces your attention.

Think of the North as a great womb. You can create the North inside your home to assist you in finding balance, a deeper connection to your body, and wisdom. Whether it's an altar to honor your ancestors or summon the spirits you are working with or a bridge to make a deeper connection to yourself and loved ones, your home can reflect your intentions.

As you work through this book and explore the North, celebrate and use your connection to nature, its connection to your body, and bring the elements and spirits into your home by charting the cardinal directions inside your home, focusing on the areas to the North.

In my home, I have one whole wall that is a living and breathing altar. It happens to be in the direction of North of my main living space. That's just the way my home was built, but your altar doesn't need to be a whole wall, nor does any main altar need to be to the North. This altar holds both the darkness of the North as well as the tranquil expression of winter in colors, stones, and earth connections. It is my North altar, the altar I dance sky-clad in front of to honor my body. I go to the North altar when I want to put my hands on my heart and squeal in unabashed joy and happiness. I celebrate at this altar and pray and sprawl out on the floor to play with my puppy. I sit in front of this altar when my body is telling me I need rest, often finding a couch close by to rest on. The floor under this altar has a soft rug, and I ground myself into the softness to give it my emotions. This altar is the one I went to in order to connect to the heartbeat of my home when it was expressing sadness that I was leaving.

You also can create a main altar, even if it's not to the North. The best place to do this is in a place where you spend a lot of time enjoying your life with your family or being with yourself. The direction of the space for a main altar that expresses you does not matter; the goal is to find a location you can connect to often and express your emotions.

Anyone who walks into that space where my main altar resides can feel the power of this altar. In fact, most people stop and gaze in front of this wall of altar space and comment on how much they love it. It's not because of how it looks; it's because of what they feel. Plus, there are a lot of books, and avid readers are mesmerized by my color-coded shelves.

In my kitchen, when tracking the directions, the North is a line of counter space where my stove resides. Above it, I have created small spaces representing the North to balance my stove's fire. Some are visible (chalice of water, flowers and plants I'm working with) and some are not (such as symbols I've painted on the walls in clear liquid, feathers inside cabinets and stones above shelves.) I've also painted small symbols on the wall that hold the sacred geometry of the earth in this sacred space of food creation and consumption.

In my office, the North is a closet that I have turned into a working altar full of magical tools, books, herbs, potions, and spell bottles. It holds the keys to my continual rebirth and growth and the ingredients for the spells I cast. Outside my house, the North has received many sacred items buried for protection and to honor the spirits I work with in that direction.

Let's do this together and start by looking to the North. Get out a compass and find which direction is North. Then look at each room's edge where the North sits. The North in your home might be a wall, contain a doorway, or be part of several rooms, and all of these spaces can be worked as the North. Work through each space and align it to how you feel in the North. Doorways have a ledge above them, and walls can hold some type of shelving. If your space has only a small section to the North and there isn't room to add anything, you can use plant allies to brush the space often and infuse it with the energy of earth. Find a small tree branch with leaves and write your intentions on them and gently run them across the wall or space to the North. There is no space to the North of your home that cannot be infused with your intentions and the element of earth.

Let's talk about the definition of an altar for a moment, as they feature prominently in rituals. An altar itself is a place you make sacred that can hold specific meaning or intention. It can be small, such as a picture on a shelf with a shell you found, or it can be an entire table devoted to prayer or ceremony. When I refer to an altar, I am referring to any space you have designated as sacred. In time you will see that all of our space is sacred, which means you can intentionally create an altar anywhere, anytime.

You are likely at the stage where you should have a strong idea of what part of the North is aligned with you or what part of your life is aligned with the North. Have that space reflect where you're at in your body and with your connection to nature. Move things around, find treasures in your home and from the earth, and add them to the North.

If the North is in the kitchen, think of how you want to feel in the kitchen. Do you want to focus on harmony with family meals? Do you want nutritious foods that support the connection to your body? Do you not like to cook but know your kitchen is a place that provides nourishment? Contemplate all these questions and decide what's right for you. Then move what you can to reflect this. There is no right or wrong, only what feels good when you are there. Then do this in each room, remaining open to the idea that what feels good will change as you continuously change.

The best way to start the process of making your space sacred is as follows:

* Open the compass on your phone and find out what direction is North in your home.
* Walk through each space, such as your kitchen, bedroom, and living room, to see what is there in the North. Is it a wall, a window, your fridge? Just take a mental note of where the North sits.

- Then grab your journal and do the walk through again and list what parts of your physical dwelling are in the North.
- Sit down with your journal and think about what you can add to the spaces that represent the element of earth.
- Some examples are: If there's a window, add a small stone above the windowsill. If there is a shelf or flat piece of furniture, add a plant or anything you find in nature. Look for any small way to represent the North in that space. The goal is to place it with intention and reverence to yourself and your connection to nature.

There are many ways to bring the North into your space, whether for your home, a temporary space such as a hotel or vacation home, or a workspace. When you see your space as a living and breathing aspect of your life, you can create the energy that supports you at any time. Bringing in the North is to bring comfort, nature, and interconnectedness into your space.

Most important, remember that your home is ever-changing, just as you are. Creating monthly rituals to determine where you are on the spiral path and where you want to be will provide you with information to create the space you desire. A good time to schedule this into your life is during the full moon. Mark your calendar and enlist family or assign it to yourself to review all directions and all altars on every full moon. Clean it, update it, and pause and hold a moment of intention.

Then you can use this information to support your endeavors in your space with intention. Your home will change if you are in tune with yourself. What you once liked in one place will shift as you move through the spiral path and experience the cycles within the cycles. Your home should and will change alongside you. The same goes for your office, workspace, outdoor space, and even the energy in your vehicle.

This is a beautiful practice to do with everyone who resides in your home. It turns chores and cleaning into a magical practice of devotion.

When my kids were young, they loved cleaning out old toys to make space for new ones. It was our family rule that before birthdays or holidays we gathered all the toys they didn't play with any longer and packaged them up and donated them for another child to enjoy. They loved the feeling of a fresh room and the dance parties we would have while cleaning and clearing old items (mainly because they knew they were about to get presents). I didn't realize it then, as I was less aware of the impact of intentional magic than I am now, but I was creating devotional rituals with my family. Rituals that, as adults, they still practice today, clearing out the old to make space for the new. My children are both masters at keeping intentional spaces clean and clear of stagnant energy, even though that was never my intention when raising them to be a part of taking care of our house together.

You know that feeling you get after cleaning your home, when it feels so fresh that your whole body feels better? We should aim for this every day in our spaces, not just on cleaning days. This can feel like a monumental task when we have busy lives with children and jobs and pets. I've been there and know it to be true. It comes down to understanding how deeply our space impacts our energy and prioritizing time to rebalance our space daily, sometimes more than once a day.

Try this the next time you feel stuck on what to do or you feel your energy is chaotic and you are not grounded; first take a look around you in that exact moment—is your office, home, room clear of clutter, and is it clean physically and energetically? If the space is not clean and tidy, do a quick sorting of the space and clean it, and I promise you the energy in your body will change immediately.

I've lived in places where I felt deeply connected to myself and the divine within me and fostered that feeling by how I cared for the space. I've also lived in spaces where I felt disconnected from myself and was processing my own internal connection (or lack thereof), which left me disconnected from the space. It's all connected and it's all sacred. When we neglect our home, it shows us where we neglect ourselves. If we are too busy to devote time to clearing and organizing, we are likely too busy to be in stillness with ourselves and aren't clearing mental clutter. By this point in the book, you know that when you don't make space and time for yourself, you'll be disconnected from your body. If you are disconnected from your body, there will be no magic or joy, let alone sacred magic, to be found.

At the heart of making spaces sacred is our intention. It can be any space—your home, office, vehicle, patch of grass, or even a temporary place like a hotel room. You are the holy of holies, and if you connect to any physical location, you can sink into its rhythm, and it can sink into you. Your physical location will change when you enter into states that feel good.

We've all crossed thresholds into others' domains and felt when their space was misaligned. Even something as simple as a couple's argument creates an energetic imprint that can be felt long after the argument has been settled. All the empty space between physical items has an entire world living in it. Wild, right? Yet true.

Wherever you are reading this, take a moment to look around. Look at the air and empty space between furniture and items. It may look empty, but it is full of energy. Pause for a moment, look at that empty space, and ask yourself, "What power does this space hold?" You'll know exactly what I'm talking about when you do this regularly.

We can create any energy we desire in any space by giving it thoughtful intention. You may have family coming for dinner, so you set the space to be loving and warm. Or if you are preparing on a Sunday for a busy week ahead, you can set up your home to support you when you return in the evenings and need to rest. Your space can and will change alongside you when you begin to work with your space and see it as sacred.

There is a shadow side to sacred space that is often neglected when discussing the intentional creation of space. This happens when you use space to dump or remove negative energy or process big emotions and don't reset the space. This can be unintentional or intentional.

Back to the couple that had a fight in their home: Imagine if that fight continues over days or weeks, sometimes years, and the negatively charged space becomes so heavy and refueled with each fight that the energy of the space takes on its own life. Which it can. People will feel it and think there is a bad spirit in the home—which there is. It's a ball of negative energy that hasn't been cleared. These balls of energy can sit in our homes and are real, and this happens often.

The good news is it's easy to change it; it only requires thoughtful intention, which is what we're doing now, even by you just reading this. I'll add several rituals in Part Two of this book that you can use to address your space.

Think of a courtroom after a murder trial. Imagine all the big emotions felt in that space by all parties, the judge, and the jury. All their emotion was felt in a closed-up space. Now picture showing up the next day in the same room for a yoga class. It would feel off and heavy or cold, like an ice bath when you expected a sauna. Space carries energy, and that is definitely not the energy you want to be in for a yoga class.

Another example is an abandoned church I came across while writing this book. It was close to a property where I was staying to focus on writing. One day, I wandered into this old church, and the moment I opened the doors, I could smell the air of people's souls. It smelled like hope, prayer, death, and possibility. I could feel the holiness of the space, and it was magical. That building had held families and prayers for more than a hundred years, and the energy was positive and loving. I spent many hours in that church, writing and enjoying the feeling. A large portion of what you are reading here was written in that abandoned church.

This is why, when you are walking the path to the holiest of all ways of life seeking magic where you experience heaven on earth, you need to address your own space. All your space, from each shadowy corner where you store unwanted clothes to the counter of your kitchen. Do not follow a recipe for what will make a happy home but create a space that fosters your own inner version of a haven.

Sacred Spaces of the North

While we are here in the stillness of the North, where both we and the earth are breathing more slowly and deeper, and we are listening to the essence of who we are, we need space to honor and reflect this period on the spiral path. It may not be your whole home or room, but it should at least be a corner where you can be still and reflect. I often call this a thinking chair. I have one, and I encourage all my students and clients to have a sacred space to go inward.

It can also be next to your bed, where you pause before sleep and reset your energy. Or even a unique altar you set up while reading this book that will hold all the parts of you that you are discovering along the way. Anything is possible; you need only to know what feels right for you.

Other books in this series will teach you how to set up threshold spaces for ceremonial magic or how to harness the power of storms for magical creation, but for now in the North, we will focus on cleansing and clearing. We honor the quiet, like the soil around a seed you hope to grow. We'll make the best soil possible for anything you create next.

Let's continue to foster the connection to your space by clearing and cleansing all facets of your dwelling. We're going to talk about cleaning next. Yes, we're going to the area most people classify as a chore. It's usually the last thing we want to do, yet we feel refreshed and settled when it's done. We usually focus on the goal of less dirt and fewer germs, but we also need to clean the energy that has settled in the form of dust in the space. When we intentionally clean our space, we turn a mundane act into a sacred process if we know that we are removing old energy and making space for fresh energy, not just for less dirt.

Whether or not you are conscious of this, it is always true. If your space is dirty or untidy, so will your energy be. So will your mind. And if your mind is unfocused and ungrounded, most likely, your space will reflect this as well.

When writers are blocked, they're taught to clean and reorganize. You're taught to reset the space when starting a new job or project. When a child goes to bed at night, we teach them to organize their room and bag for school—these are all practices to ensure your space is set up for success.

How you define order versus chaos in your space is very personal. Tidy and clean are two things; organization is a personal preference. Even as I write this chapter, I look around and see a giant bristol board on an easel with color-coded notes, a big binder of notes spread out around me, two journals, a pad of sticky notes, and several snacks and drinks. It may appear chaotic to some, but it is perfectly organized for me. It's clean and tidy for me. As I progressed in the book and the creation stage came to a close, and I began to focus on rewriting and editing, all the chaos was taken down, and I had only a cup of something to drink and my reading glasses nearby. My space changes for the stage of the project I'm working on.

Let your spaces be unique to you.

We'll start with getting rid of old items you no longer need. Go through your house and fill one box weekly with items you no longer use or want. This is considerable work, so take it slow. After you fill the box, separate it between donation and trash. Keep doing this until you can no longer fill a box. Clearing out what you no longer need can sometimes takes weeks or months. You should do this one box at a time until you love and connect with everything left in your home, then you know you are done. Note that you will be done removing clutter only for now and should return to this quarterly, as things will immediately begin to accumulate again.

Turn on music you like moving your body to and dance while you clean and discard old items. Make it a magical party of cleaning and organizing. This brings your body, energy, and emotion into the experience. Use the yes/no ritual listed earlier if you aren't sure what to keep or what to give away (or throw away).

Next set aside time each week in devotion to your dwelling. Whether it's a small studio or a large house, devote one part of one day each week to your space. This is the time to clean and tidy your space. Regular cleaning, knowingly or not, is always a devotional practice. Looking at it this way, it becomes less of a chore and more of a magical practice of setting the tone for how you want to feel in your space.

Sacred Spaces of the North

That's the task, and once you master this, you will start to feel your space return that devotion to you. In addition to regular cleaning, stop in each corner of your space, close your eyes, and ask yourself how it feels. Do the same with closets and spaces you do not use often. If they feel stale or void of energy, infuse them with items that feel magical. At the very least, clean and organize them. We often think that closing a door to a closet that is cluttered will block it off from the house, yet this isn't true. All parts of your house are connected as one ball of energy and each part matters.

You may also wish to regularly complete a ritual smoke cleanse of your space after you've cleaned. I will provide the exact steps on how to do a cleansing ritual in Part Two, including alternatives if you cannot use smoke. Witch or not, regularly working with plant allies as described in the previous chapter is a way to utilize the medicinal properties of plants through smoke cleansing. The ritual of burning a specific plant to clear and infuse your space (and your energy) has been done for thousands of years because it works.

Here's how this will look.

1. Clear out everything in your home that you no longer need or want. Start this now and continue it as long as needed, one box at a time. Buh-bye old energy!
2. Then add to your schedule a weekly time in devotion to your space, whether it's an hour or a day. Make this a habit and a ritual. This time is to clean and take time in each and every corner to see how it feels. More old energy will be gone, gone, gone.
3. Complete a smoke-clearing ritual of your home once it's clear to open the space and fill it with the energy you desire.
4. Clear and cleanse altars and special places in your home on every full moon, recharging the items or moving them to adjust to your month ahead. Aah, magic moves into the space.

Sacred Magic

This is powerful work to find the North in your home, create a representation of the element of earth in all places in your home, then learn to dedicate time and attention to devotion to the connection between you and your space. It is a sacred practice and once you bring this ritual into your life, every moment you are in the space will feel very different. You'll master the idea that you can change how you feel just by the simple commitment to taking care of your space. It holds you. It's an extension of you. And like a great womb, it will become fertile ground for whatever you desire in your life.

Contemplation questions

1. In what area of my home do I feel the most joy? Why?

2. In what area do I spend the most time? Why?

3. What area feels heavy so I avoid it? Explore this further.

4. Now think of your home as its own energy field and ask yourself, "How does my home itself want to feel?"

5. What type of sanctuary and feelings do I want to have when I walk into my home?

6. When can I plan a weekly devotional to my home to cleanse and set the space to how I want to feel?

Chapter Eight
Dreaming in the North

WHILE WE ARE IN THE NORTH, we are exploring how the earth element, plants, our body, winter, and our spaces create and impact the energy we live and breathe. Another important facet to the path of sacred magic is what happens in dreamtime.

Entire new worlds can be experienced while we are sleeping. Worlds open and our emotions, fears, and possibilities become places we visit while our mind is resting and our spirit is free to play and explore. Dreamtime is a sacred time; not only is it a time when our body and mind are still, but it's also a time when our human, conditioned beliefs are at rest. When conditioned beliefs are at rest, the mysteries of life can be explored without the restraints of what we've been told is possible.

I'll share with you a time when short periods of sleep completely transformed my life, when the spirit world cracked wide open while my eyes were shut.

I lay on the small pebbles of black sand without another soul in sight. I felt the heat on my skin and could smell the saltiness of the ocean's waves a few feet away. My body was achy from the long walk to find this secret place, and I rested my head on my backpack. I was in Hawaii for a three-month stay, and I had wandered long and far to find this place on one of my days of adventuring.

When I first arrived in this sacred place, I had spoken the words of a ritual called Beauty Way. Its body movements and words honor the beauty within and without. I love to do this ritual in spaces and times when I want to say thank you to the lands.

It started with facing North and saying, "Beauty in front of me, beauty behind me, beauty to the right of me, beauty to the left of me, beauty above me, beauty below me, beauty inside me." Then I made a quarter turn to a new direction and repeated the saying until all four directions received this blessing.

I completed the blessing and sat down on the deserted pebbled beach and rested. As I closed my eyes, I repeated the ritual in my mind, not because I wanted to do more ritual but because it was so beautiful that I couldn't stop speaking the words. I wasn't expecting to fall so deeply asleep, and I certainly wasn't expecting what happened next.

As I drifted off into the dreamscape that felt like it had become a fantasy of swirling colors all around me, three people came into my dream. They all had dark hair, and one was bouncing up and down with a smile on her face. The second kept her sunglasses on and filed her nails in uninterest, and the third was almost holographic, and I couldn't decipher anything about her. They danced in the colors around me, and I felt it all in my body, even while sleeping. There was nothing else of significance to this dream, and it felt like they had come for a visit and were quickly gone again.

Dreaming in the North

When I opened my eyes, my body was even more tired, the type of tiredness you feel after sleeping in the sun. It felt like it had been only a few minutes, but when I checked my phone, I was amazed that more than an hour had passed. I had no idea who or why these three goddess-type figures had visited me while resting. And I had never seen a being in my dreams filing her nails. I smiled in the wonder of it all and set it aside. I stripped down and cooled off in the ocean before I wrote in my journal about the three visitors I had in my dream. Nothing more stood out from the experience so my journal entry about it was short and more focused on the beauty of the secret place I had found while adventuring.

I continued on my day of hiking and exploring, leaving the experience in my journal without further thought.

A few days later, when I was back inside the small cottage in the rainforest I was calling home for a few months, I had a session booked with a massage therapist who is also a master energy worker and psychic. She had been coming every two weeks since I arrived and was part of how I was taking care of myself while immersing myself deeply on this solo quest in Hawaii.

As she unfolded the legs of the table and smoothed out blankets, she looked sideways at me and said, "Ah, I see that you have had new spirits visiting you since I saw you last." I didn't know who she was referring to, as it was a wild and magical time, and I had many new spirits visiting me during my stay in Hawaii as the lands themselves were very spiritual. I just said "yes" and smiled.

Once I settled on the table and she smoothed the blankets on top of me, she said again that the visitors had been waiting for me for a long time. Her words hummed through my body, and I felt like I was floating while I mostly focused on quieting my mind in anticipation of a great massage.

I still did not connect what she was saying and what had occurred a few days before. I was communicating with lands and sinking deeply into the circadian rhythms, so it all felt magical. It was an impactful combination of the powerful lands of Hawaii and the small, one-room dwelling that I had made my own, plus the removal of outside noise and people. I was heavily immersed in my world and the spiritual plane. Although I continued to do my work virtually while there, the first month after I arrived, I didn't interact with others except to get supplies and occasionally speak to the woman who had offered me the space.

The complete removal of city life and noise was changing me daily by opening senses that had long been dormant; even in my magical practices, I had never felt as attuned to nature as I was during that time. I was in that portal of awe the whole time and the connection she made seemed part of one big experience. Her comments about these spirits were just another one of the confirmations of what I was experiencing daily.

As she began to massage my body and infuse it with healing energy, I drifted off to sleep again. The three spirits from my previous dream appeared. The one bounced in glee again, the second one took her glasses off, and the third hovered behind them. I could feel their entire focus on me. They were there for me. I felt my pulse quickening and immediately woke up just as the healer asked me to turn over. Again, almost an hour had gone by when it felt like just a few minutes.

She said, "Our spirit guides can take on different forms when we are in different lands, but the new ones that have appeared have come now, as it is the time for them to begin their work." I didn't speak. I felt in my belly that what she had said was true. I didn't ask any questions; I didn't need to. I felt the truth in the electrical vibration that was pulsing through me.

When she was finished and we sat down to talk, I explained what I had experienced and how I didn't realize what she had been referring to until the spirits came into my dream again. She confirmed that she could feel that I had a new energy source around me since she had been there last, and they had spoken to her.

The three new guides remain with me and come only when I dream. Sometimes I can recall if there was anything specific, but often I remember only them being there. They come together, and I spend time contemplating what I was thinking of in my life then; that's where I find their messages. I like it when they come, as it's a reminder of a time in my life that was very special, and their visit brings that energy to whatever I'm facing at the moment. I continue to thank them with an offering of a small plate of flowers and one of the stones I collected while in Hawaii.

Hundreds of books and resources are available to anyone who wants to explore the depths of their subconscious and superconscious mind, which appear only when we are stripped bare of the masks and pretenses we spend many of our waking hours engulfed in. If this area interests you, then go deep. Find books, podcasts, and videos to learn more about how programming inside your mind plays out when you close your eyes.

That's not what I'm going to cover here. Instead, we are going to look at how being in the North will impact your dreams and how they are powerful times of messages. And I'll show you how to use dreaming in the North to cultivate a deeper understanding of where you are in the moment of your soul path and what spirits are assisting you. When you let your mind rest and turn off the filter that processes everything you are carrying in your body, your dreams will lead you further into yourself.

There are two common questions about dreams I want to address up front. First, what happens if I cannot remember my dreams? Do not worry; this is common. I will share rituals at the end of the book that will help you increase the chances of remembering more details, but mostly I want you to know that you shouldn't force it. What comes and remains will be enough. Second, what happens if I don't dream? There are several answers to this question, but most of the time, this can be explained by looking at your sleep habits, medications, and how disconnected you may be from your body. You often dream, even if you do not remember it the next day.

In the world of dreams of the North, time stands still or moves at the pace of a garden snail. When time stands still, it's because we are actually collapsing timelines and experiencing the past, present, and future in one wild landscape called dreams.

> **When you find yourself in the North and dreaming**, you experience dreams that are related to where you are not allowing yourself enough space to slow down, to ponder what is right for you at that moment, and to see how you are or not connected to your body. This is also the time land spirits and ancestors will visit you.

> **When you are in the East and dreaming**, you will experience scenes where your fears and beliefs are challenged and will explore other ways of thinking that can be tried on for size. You may visit with your spirit guides, angels, or archangel energies.

> **When you find yourself in the South and dreaming**, you will process your unresolved anger or passions that you hide from the world. You express yourself and hidden desires when in the South.

> **If you are in the West and dreaming**, you will experience the feelings of floating, of movement, of change, and possibly even of moving between the worlds of spirit and human. Water spirits and deep-level emotions often show themselves in our dreams when we are in the West as a gentle invitation to bring them into our human lives.

Time bends and weaves, creating a landscape where past, present, and future blur together in a colorful collage when we are sleeping. We can call upon the North before we sleep to bring in symbols and understanding. We can ride the tree's roots deeper and heal if healing is needed.

We can honor the silence within ourselves while we rest. We can set intentions for the most significant connection we seek here in the North, the connection to our body. We can set this intention, and cells and working parts of our body that connect to our intentions will support this sacred desire while sleeping.

We enter the astral plane in dreamtime when we are in the North to connect to our ancestors and beings from the spiritual world, to find out why we are here in the North, and to learn what inward-facing wisdom wants to be brought into our wakeful hours.

We're going to look at this in two ways. First, we'll explore what happens to our dreams when entrenched in the North when the earth seems to be holding its breath in anticipation of our upcoming rebirth. This is when we've come to the North knowing we can find solitude and stability and where whispering pines and silent snowfalls become the nurturing we need. Second, we will learn how to create bedtime rituals to open portals into the unseen realms and sink deeper into the North where we'll explore methods for deciphering the messages we receive.

To start understanding what happens in our dreamtime when in the North, we need to understand if life itself put us in the North or if we chose to move ourselves into this place on the spiral path. We need to understand why because it will impact how we interpret what we are dreaming about.

Let's look at a few examples; if you have experienced a shake-up in your life or a trauma you haven't fully processed (with talk therapy or rituals) and you just keep keepin' on with life, you are definitely still in the North, and this stuck energy or shadow that was created inside you will come out in your dreams. Healing takes time and healing means bringing the issue to the surface and letting it be seen, felt, and moved. Trauma or a life shake-up never comes at a convenient time when we can stop everything and feel it and process it with long days of rest, which means we spend a lot of our time pushing it down because we don't have the time to actually process it. One of the ways this presents itself is that it becomes hard to fall asleep or stay asleep. Our mind is desperately trying to connect the feelings to our body, and when we lie down and try to sleep, it can come tumbling through us like a freight train. Then dreams will be the last thing on our mind. It's OK to set any of life's shake-ups aside for moments of time but not for long or it will build up and become toxic. One way to address this is to write it out before bedtime.

Write it by saying, "This thing happened that I'm not happy about. I don't know how I feel yet or how to process it yet, but I'm leaving it here for the moment to carry on with what I need to do and will come back to it soon. I am safe to leave it here and let my mind and body rest." You can practice grounding daily while you are still processing any big feelings, so you can leave them behind when you need sleep.

Another way to know you are in the North in your dreams is by the spirits that come to you. It's interesting to know that most people, in my experience, when they dream of family members (ancestors) who have passed, have visions of people walking in the forest, or experience any scene or movement set outdoors, it's a sign the spirits are walking with you at the time. These are North dreams, as they are connected to the element of earth and connected to your body (your bloodline).

In this case the best way to decipher why or what is being shared with you is to create a simple bedtime altar to capture the information and open the lines of communication in the daytime. Note here that you are always in control. If you do *not* want spirits to visit you in your dreams (in any direction), speak aloud before sleep that no visitors are allowed while your eyes are closed. You get to choose.

But if you do want to strengthen the connection while sleeping, try the following.

1. Once the first dream (or contact) has happened, write down everything you can remember or even just the words, "I know you visited me, and you are welcome to come again."

Dreaming in the North

2. Keep this journal right next to where you sleep so each day when you wake up, you can write out any insights before you actually get out of bed (which is the most powerful way to remember your dreams).
3. Create a small altar of items that represent your ancestors or nature around you, such as family mementos, pictures, listed names, or anything from earth if it is an earth spirit. Add a small glass of water (you will not drink this) to aid the connection while sleeping and to filter out bad vibrations. Add flowers or items that represent beauty so the relationship during dreamtime is built on a budding connection.
4. Practice deep belly breathing before sleep, and as you drift off, speak to whomever is visiting you and say that you welcome the visit and their insight and knowledge.
5. Continue writing out your dreams the next day.
6. You should do this for at least one week if you want to really understand who and what is connecting with you and what they want you to know.

When we are entrenched in the North, our dreams will take on a whole new energetic feel. Your dreams might feel heavier, you might sleep deeper, or you might see yourself covered or inside dark places. Do you allow this to create fear in your body? You shouldn't. If you know you are in the North, the enclosure of your dreams is like a womb, and the womb is a place of refuge and restoration. The most important thing to do when you know you are in the North and entering into dreamtime is to fully release what the experiences have been on that day so you can rest.

Sleep is one of the most important parts of spending time on the spiral path to the North, and focusing on clearing anything out of your energy field before you sleep is the way to do it.

Whether you've chosen to take yourself to the North for rest and recovery, to process deep emotions, or to take a sacred pause, let everything else go and give your mind permission to turn off and let your body be free to feel and experience rest.

Another way to approach dreams while in the North is to make them intentional. You can take your intentions, goals, or desires and add them to your bedtime rituals to allow the power of the great womb that comes while dreaming in the North to nurture you and your intentions.

For example, when you are in the North yet also trying to work big manifesting rituals, your intentions during dreamtime should be for healing, removing blocks, or shining light on where your energy is heavy. Focusing on removing blocks or shining light on what you cannot see in waking hours will greatly aid your manifestations. Again, keeping a journal by your bed to write down anything that comes to you while sleeping is important.

Another example I often see is when someone is in denial that they are still processing something big that happened in their life (or even just in that one day) and they haven't given themselves time to handle it and get grounded into their body. They feel floaty and out of control and don't know what to do with the big energy they are feeling. It can be a big happy event or a painful event, or everything in between. They all require time to think about them, feel them, celebrate them, or weep over them—anything that feels right that allows your body to acknowledge the big energy. When we ignore it, our body will process it when our mind, the great blocker of self-serving truth, is turned off. If you go into dreamtime with big energy that hasn't been processed, you are going to experience dreams that are related to what has not been processed.

The key to dreaming as a way to experience the full spectrum of spirits and magic in the North is to process the real human experiences you have each day and clear and ground them before you go to sleep. This allows for a fresh and peaceful sleep or a deeply profound spiritual sleep.

There is one more major influence on our sleep that needs to be addressed. You've probably heard at some point in your adult life that digital media will greatly impact your dreams and the quality of your sleep. If you scroll social media for an hour before bed then sleep with your phone still on with alerts and buzzing going off, nothing I am going to teach you will matter. What you do on your phone and what you allow into your field are louder influences than any ritual or spell.

In the sacredness of the North, time feels slower and dreams take on a whole new rooted, sacred life of their own. We recess inward to seek sustenance and rest from our internal chase of the digital world and the hamster wheel we find ourselves on. Therefore, put your phone away well before you go to bed. Tune out the digital noise so it doesn't become the ritual you have inadvertently put into place before you sleep. If the last thing you saw on your screen was something that didn't feel good, that's what you will be taking into the dream realm. Stop doing that! Also, if you are working or checking email before bed, you are taking work into your hours of rest and recovery. Stop this too; no job or work task is worth taking away your precious hours of sleep.

I have included a full digital detox in Part Two of this book. Before I tell you how to work with magic to improve your dreams, I must tell you that if you do not detach from digital noise before you enter dreamtime (in any stage or place on the spiral path), nothing will improve your dreams. It's simple really—turn your phone notifications off and put your phone away to charge an hour before bed. You can program your phone to allow favorites to break through if you are concerned about family being able to reach you. Other than that, everything else can wait. This is not a negotiable area when it comes to dreamtime if you are walking this path.

Even better, spend that hour before bed when your phone (and all electronics) is off to journal, read a book, do breathwork, practice grounding, or connect to your body. Part Two has many options you can choose from to fill this time before sleep. When you do intentional rituals before bed every night, your entire experience in dreamtime will change.

Now that you've spent this much time exploring the North, use the answers to any of the contemplation questions to create a bedtime ritual. This intention could include improved connection to the element of earth or spirit guides, your body, working with a specific plant ally, healing, or anything you have been pondering or have learned so far. Just try it; don't wait until you finish the book or master any type of magic. Start with turning off all devices an hour before sleep and fill that hour with something that makes you feel better as a whole.

If you are calling in more earth, groundedness, and connection to your body, bring an earth plant ally to bed with you, write an intention on a piece of paper, and place it around the plant. Or write it on the leaf of the plant itself in marker. Try ivy, moss, comfrey, patchouli, a root vegetable, or a small tree branch. You can put more than one plant in a small mesh bag or tie branches or stalks with a ribbon. Another option is to set an intention to bring balance by writing it out on a small paper circle and tying it to the plant. If it's a small enough part of a plant and written intention, you can even put it under your pillow while you sleep. Leave it until the balance has been restored and the dreamtime magic has worked, then give the item back to the earth and bury your paper.

If you are calling in a greater connection to your ancestors, make a small ancestral altar space near your bed and add a written intention asking them to visit while you sleep. I'll share more details on how to create altars in Part Two.

Regardless of what you desire to experience in the North—releasing, honoring, or connecting—you can create an intention around it that will be near you while you sleep. Let any physical items or written desires work magic while you travel between the realms. Again (and I'll say this on repeat), always keep a dream journal next to your bed to either hold the intentions of what you wish to experience while sleeping or for you to note down what you remember from your dreams when you wake up.

When people ask me to help them decipher their dreams, I start by asking what is currently stressing or perplexing them, how they are addressing it, and how it feels in their body. Then we go into their bedtime rituals.

Dreaming in the North

If you want your dreamtime to be filled with knowledge and good rest, as with everything in this book, it's about putting intentions into it and committing to making change to improve your life. The more you improve your life and your connection to all facets of your soul, mind and body, the closer you are getting to experiencing heaven on earth. That's the whole point of finding sacred magic.

Contemplation questions

1. I remember a dream once that rocked me; it was?

2. I don't remember my dreams when?

3. I want to dream more about?

4. My new evening rituals will be?

5. How can I set up my morning ritual to better record my dreams?

6. My beliefs about my dreams are?

Chapter Nine
Psychic Gifts

WE FEEL MORE THAN WE SPEAK. We know more than we admit to anyone. Deep down, if you really think about it, you'll recall times when you knew something would happen before it did.

It's a lifetime of work to unravel why we need to keep what we know hidden, even from ourselves. I've known many things to be true in my core and yet took no action, not even acknowledging the knowing to myself. We are not alone in this, as it's been beaten out of us by mainstream media and the boxes society wants us to fit into, not to mention the definition of "psychic" that has been fed to us from television (where the goal is to tell you their vision). In school, we were not taught how to use our intuition or natural empathic gifts to make decisions. Instead, we were taught to do it one way—to fall in line and achieve the grade. Yet the wonder of looking back and realizing we knew far more than we were willing to acknowledge is a practice we can engage in to deepen our connection to the unseen worlds. I know you know, and I also understand why you doubt what you know. If we cannot confirm what we feel or know to be true, we ignore it. We ignore it if it means changing our lives because of what we know. There are many reasons for this, yet we can choose to use this knowledge more meaningfully.

I'm going to answer your most burning question right here: YES, everyone has access to psychic gifts. You might know it as "intuition" or "I just had a feeling" or "I knew you were going to say that." It's all the same starting place, and in this section we are going to take that starting place that is innate (meaning we're born with it) to all of us and focus on developing and increasing our extra senses.

Before I had the tools to use my gifts as part of my practice for myself and eventually for others, there was one specific time when my spiritual and psychic gifts profoundly came through my body and I ignored them as long as I could.

Remember the story I shared earlier about writing my memoir and reliving an entire painful experience to capture it for my book? There is another part of the story that I'll tell you about now.

Weeks before the most painful moments of that stage in my life, I knew something wasn't right in my relationship with my husband. I could feel it in my belly when I was with my family. My husband acted the same, but something was off. My body felt it; at first, I didn't understand, and later, I didn't want to understand. If I'm honest now when looking back, I had felt this strange inner knowing for months.

He didn't speak to my kids or me any differently. We still saw our friends and attended community events and had parties in the backyard. We read stories to the kids together, yet I couldn't shake the feeling. I had no proof or information to understand it, but slowly, the thoughts came into my mind telling me something wasn't right. I had asked him several times in several different ways if everything was OK, and his response was always, "Yes, everything is fine," but my belly remained unsettled.

One cold and rainy October morning, as I was getting dressed in my walk-in closet, I could hear the kids awake in their rooms and my husband in the shower. As I went to pull on a soft, oversize sweater with extra-long sleeves and thumb holes, I knocked something off the shelf, his cell phone. At the time, cell phones were the flip-open kind and when his fell, it flipped open.

I looked down and what I saw on the screen of his phone was the beginning of the end of my marriage. The screen showed four missed calls from one of my best friends. I didn't want to, but I scrolled through his call history and saw weeks of hour-long phone calls between him and my friend.

I knew what I knew. But my mind couldn't process it and said, "No way this is happening."

I slowly walked into the bathroom, after returning the phone to where it was supposed to be hidden in the closet, and asked my husband through the shower steam when he had last spoken to my friend. He answered, "A few months ago."

I knew what I knew, but now my heart said, "No, please, no." Even with proof, my heart still didn't want this to be true.

Then I remembered a friend whose parents had gone through several affairs and her mom had hired a private investigator. I left my body completely when I made the call and hired him.

He was a kind man who met me on a back road in our town, and I paid him cash to get the answers that ended that phase of my life. When I told him what I had felt for weeks and what I had recently found, he responded, "You know what you know. I'll get you proof, but you already know." Three days later, the investigator called me to join him where he had been staked out watching my husband. He had caught them in a car together and invited me to come and have the opportunity to confront the situation.

In retrospect, I know that I knew something wasn't right for a long time. I didn't want to believe it, so I shut it down and tried to ignore it. One of the golden nuggets of wisdom I take from that time is the deep knowing I had but didn't listen to. When we don't listen to the first signs, they tend to come barreling in stronger, as was the case when I found his cell phone.

Spiritual and psychic gifts come with the warning that once you know, you can't unknow. When your gifts become more activated, you'll learn deep and reflective truths about yourself and others. Knowing doesn't always mean acting immediately or burning down your life. When you gain knowing, it only means knowledge. Knowledge becomes the power you use to make critical decisions in your life. But yes, sometimes it means burning it down, as I did once I finally accepted what I could no longer deny.

Similarly, years later, I randomly received a strong, intuitive nudge to start my podcast. Having zero experience didn't stop me. By then I knew the feeling had meaning, and I knew how to listen to the message that my intuitive gifts were giving me. I knew I was meant to do it without any rational thought or reasoning as to why. I have long since learned to listen to the inner knowings I have; they have never, not even once, led me astray from my path. By that point, I had learned to listen and was already doing the work outlined in this book. This time I listened even when it didn't make sense, but that didn't mean it was easy.

Even when people in my inner circle laughed at my idea, I still listened and didn't let the knowing leave me. I also knew it was about more than who would listen or care. It was an opportunity for me to grow, share, and awaken my voice. I could feel this to be true in my body because I knew when my body had a reaction that felt like "Oh, this is going to matter." That much I knew, even though I quivered at the idea of hitting "record" and sitting in front of a microphone by myself. If there's one thing I know about the things that make my quiver, it's that they teach me a ton of wisdom. I followed the intuitive feeling, shaking the whole time.

I began consuming everything I could learn about podcasting, including the equipment, what systems to use, and how to be a good interviewer. Still quivering at the thought, I repeatedly asked myself if I were really going to start a podcast.

I took it slow and learned how podcasting works, then moved to how to be a good interviewer, and tried (am still trying) to understand the equipment itself. All the while I was wondering what this was all about.

Then one day I did it. I went into my closet (the only quiet place in my home), held up the microphone, and hit the record button. My face was hot, and I was sweating profusely by the time I was done.

My first show was recorded. Looking back, I still shudder at how awful I sounded.

I carried on, jumping in feet first into the podcast adventure and learned as I went. I started with the focus of supporting women in business and exploring the challenges women face when becoming solo business owners. I was learning while I was sharing by featuring top female experts along the way. What I didn't know at the time was that I was learning to speak my truth publicly, which I now do easily, without quivering, on very large platforms and social media. The process trained me, opened my throat chakra, and became a stepping stone to what I do now as a witch.

It started with a strong urge to do something I had never done before. I surrendered and said, "OK, I'll do this." And I did, even though I quivered and shook a lot along the way. If I hadn't listened to that first strong nudge to start a podcast in the first place, I certainly wouldn't have been ready to talk about being a witch on my show years later. One thing led to another, which led to my growth, which led to another knowing. And this is still the case with my show.

With over 400 episodes released (across all the shows I've hosted or guest-hosted), years of growth, and countless guest appearances, I have never forgotten that my inner knowing and psychic gift created this. I know that feeling when it is a nudge in one direction or another, and I now never, ever ignore it.

I receive knowledge all day about what's happening in nature around me, in the trees, in the plants inside my home, and inside my own life. My body is constantly receiving information, and I need only to slow my breath and open myself to receive in order to gain the knowledge. One indoor plant in my home communicates with me occasionally, sending thoughts that pop into my mind, telling me it wants more water. My psychic gifts inform me when to launch a new program or open space for one-on-one clients. My inner knowledge guides me on the direction to take in business. I also use my spiritual gifts to determine what would nourish my body, what foods to eat, and what to read or listen to. My gifts and inner knowing guide each moment of my life. When I'm super busy and have overbooked myself, I'll know because my knowing fields will be quiet, and I'll be reminded to take time to breathe and focus on slowing down. When I slow down, I can determine what is off and what is aligned, and if I need to change direction.

This is another example of when you go slow, you become steady. When you become steady, the information moves smoothly. When information comes in smooth, then you can go fast. Slow is steady, steady becomes smooth, and smooth is fast.

You can do this, too, and I will teach you. But to do so, you must be willing to remain undefined for a little longer and move slowly with me into the spiritual realm and activate your gifts. This quest we are on together will help you learn to listen to what is always available to you, and I promise you it's worth it. Inside your body lives a well of knowledge that I call your psychic gifts. Your unique gifts are part of what is sacred and magical about you.

This knowledge is where you find the remembering that you are in control and get to choose how you want to live. Using your gifts isn't just about looking ahead to predict the future; it's also about knowing how to use your gifts to determine what is right for you in this exact moment. It's tapping into the energy that is all around you to feel what is happening and make decisions based on what you feel.

I can look at the weather and see all the sunny skies ahead, and yet inside my body I can tell if a low-pressure system is coming. Nature tells me what is coming, the smell in the air tells me what is coming, and my body slows down and tells me what is coming. I can feel it in all my senses, which are constantly bringing information into my body.

As we have delved deeply into the North, we have seen it is the place of connection to our body. When we explore our spiritual gifts, we can see that they all come through our body, regardless of what label or name we give them.

To learn how to use your psychic gifts, we'll start by working with your five senses since your gifts come through your body. For example, if you want to work on clairvoyance (clear seeing), you can develop this by improving how you interpret signs, signals, light, and movement with your physical eyes. Your eyes take in a large amount of data every second of the day, yet that is only a small fraction of what is actually occurring around you. You cannot see your cell phone signal or your internet rays, yet you know they are there. If you practice visual exercises based on what your eyes see and learn to experience it in your mind's eye, you will create an imprint on your eyelids when your eyes are closed. From there, you can see with your mind's eye even when your eyes are open. They become one field of knowledge, both the physical eye and the mind's eye. This process is possible through all your senses, and it *all* comes through the body.

Each book in this series on the spiral path will have direct connections to the gifts that lie in that direction. You do not need to wait until a painful experience forces you into reflection to admit that you knew; you can learn how to develop and trust your gifts in very simple and easy to use ways. Once you learn the basics and you know how your gifts work, you can continue to develop them until they are strong and accessible anytime. Just like with a muscle in your body, repetitions are required for growth.

Working with your psychic gifts will deeply impact your career and relationships. Your gifts will show you how to navigate changes in your life, from simple choices like which restaurant will have a shorter wait time when deciding where to eat for dinner to more complication decisions, such as what job to apply for, when to make a change in a relationship, and, of course, where to follow the golden path to making more money. Your psychic gifts won't show you the lottery numbers; they'll show you the steps to take along the spiral path to create a better life based on what YOU (yes, you) ultimately want.

I will warn you now that you won't always get it right when you begin this work, nor will you know what to actually do with the knowledge once your gifts begin delivering truth to you. Your mind will resist (as mine did) if what you learn from your gifts feels scary. You'll wonder what people think of you when you start making decisions based on your inner knowledge or psychic gifts. You'll meet resistance from your family and friends if you follow your gifts and the knowledge you receive. Most people will not accept the answers of "This just feels right to me" or "Something feels off to me so I'm not going to do that."

I understand this will be challenging, and I encourage you to embrace the unknown and follow your gifts as they come in, even if it makes no sense to anyone else. Let yourself be amazed at how deeply your body can connect to wisdom. Even when it's hard, knowing you carry that much power inside you puts you back in the driver's seat of your life.

While we are here in the North questing for sacred magic, remember that all the experiences, beliefs, and traumas that live in your body will fog the lens you use to interpret the information you receive. These are spiritual blind spots.

Take me as an example. My life changed when I went through the painful unraveling of my marriage. Since then, when I'm doing readings or magical workings for anyone else and there is a question of an affair with my client or their partner, my lens will always have a slightly skewed viewpoint. I work very hard to clear this field so I can use my gifts without my own trauma fogging the lens. It remains an area that I am conscious of and one I need to put in extra effort into to ensure my field is clear when it comes up. I've been known to turn down clients or readings if I don't have a clear field and I sense a blind spot appearing. It's rare now, as I've done the work and have experienced so many different types of relationships that the idea of infidelity no longer holds a

Psychic Gifts

charge in my body. But following the affair and activation of my gifts, I traveled carefully to check on how skewed my vision could be.

It is the same with how we perceive the information we receive for ourselves. Throughout our lives, we've had experiences that have formed beliefs about what's possible. Our psychic gifts often challenge those beliefs, showing us something entirely different. To see the knowledge through the lens of what's possible versus what you've experienced previously takes time and deep self-awareness to remain open to new ways of being.

As an example, one of the common parts of our gifts that most people can access is clear seeing, or clairvoyance. When our seer vision is activated, our gifts often show us symbols as a way of giving us messages. Imagine in your mind a stop sign. We all know what that looks like and if you were pondering a decision to do something or not and you saw a stop sign, you would say, "Oh, the intuitive knowing I see is a no." Now imagine if when you were a teenager that you missed a stop sign when you first learned to drive and ended up getting into an accident, you might interpret the stop sign as "I missed something." We all have experiences that will guide us in how we receive information.

Our minds, beliefs, and life experiences change the filtering system of the information we receive. To have a clean filter for knowledge to come through without it being skewed by old beliefs or false ideas, keep working on yourself and your complete body, mind, and spirit. Learn to understand yourself and heal your shadows. Connect to your body more and more and the lens through which you receive information will become clearer and clearer.

I have a student in mystery school who is a gifted spirit walker with many spirits that come to her in visions and during waking hours. She leads a successful career and manages thousands of employees. Coming from a religious family, she has been conditioned to fear the devil and hell, seeing the underworld as something to avoid at all costs. She fears that going into the underworld might bring physical death. She's done extensive work to shed those beliefs, but they linger.

When she sees dead people or something from the underworld calling her for clearing and healing, she immediately classifies them as angels, archangels, or spirit guides. That's the lens through which she receives information because she carries trauma from her religious conditioning. She cannot see clearly, let alone name aloud that a dead person came to her with a message.

In this case, it makes no difference what she names it or how she classifies the spirit that comes to her. She can only do what feels comfortable to her. What she has learned to do in an amazing way for her to lead her employees and her life is to listen to the core message she is receiving and not focus on where it came from. She is a great listener to the spirits who talk to her, and they guide her life and leadership every single day. The labels don't matter; the ability to listen and use the knowledge does.

Before we proceed, I want to share my expertise in developing gifts in others. I've taught thousands of people how to turn on their gifts and recognize their presence in their lives. One thing I know to be true is that it is never as cut and dried as traditional psychic development teaches. We are unique, and our gifts often come in rare and super-magically combined ways. Just like your fingerprint is unique to you, your psychic gifts are unique.

You may hear your name called randomly when no one is around yet feel mostly connected as a seer (this is a combination of clairaudient—clear hearing—and clairvoyant). You may have belly-level solid intuition with sparks of colors in your peripheral vision (claircognizant—clear knowing—and clairvoyant). You might be highly sensitive to energy around you and feel pulsing in your third eye when someone is lying. On it goes into any possible combination of sensing and extra-sensing. We are unique, and our gifts never, and I mean never, fall into an exact category. Nor do they work the same way as anyone else's gifts.

Here's where it gets fun: When you are swirling into your magic, your psychic gifts will change and flex the deeper you sink into the connection between nature and your body. They will expand as you learn to connect to plants, sacred spaces, and dreamtime. You'll see, feel, and know that everything around and inside you is connected. You'll feel it deeply in your human physical senses then notice your extra senses also begin to awaken.

Many people wonder if they have the magic inside them that allows them to receive messages from the unseen worlds, because they cannot tick the box of how gifts are explained. They certainly do. The labels and teachings we give for how your psychic gifts *might* work are only a starting point. Everyone has psychic gifts, and everyone can learn to develop them more.

Your human eyes can see more than just what's in front of you if you choose to learn how, but it will require you to shed old beliefs about the word "psychic." You probably visualize an old hippie lady looking over a crystal ball, which couldn't be further from the truth. The top business experts in the world will tell you that they know how to work with what "feels" right at any given time. They may not use the terms I'm using, but make no mistake—high achievers all know how to use their intuition to guide them on their path of success. Your human ears can hear more than just the noise in your physical space when you learn to hear in different vibrational ways. Your body can feel so much more than your mind can know when you learn to connect to your body and listen.

We can all receive information through our body from the spiritual realm, nature, other humans, and energy itself. We can commune with those who have passed on from this lifetime. We all have the magical superpower to hear, see, know, feel, and taste. It's a matter of learning how your body works and practicing.

It really is that simple. So now that I've added that strong caveat to what I'll share next, remember that you will likely not fit into a particular area or box of knowing. You are a unique combination that only you can know. These are merely ways to explain how your gifts can work, one at a time, but note that yours will be several of them in various ways; let yourself be unique and explore all the ways your senses are alive.

Here is a list of all commonly labeled psychic gifts. We will then explore the ones specific to the North.

Clairvoyance: This is the ability to perceive events, information, or objects beyond the normal senses and is often called "clear seeing." Clairvoyants may see visions, images, or symbols in their mind's eye or even perceive them externally. This can be in black-and-white pictures or in color. They may be flashes of light, or it could run like a video. Clairvoyants often do not know it is happening, as it has always been that way for them. Many don't realize their visual superpower isn't present for all humans.

Clairaudience: This is the ability to hear sounds or voices beyond the physical realm. Clairaudient individuals may hear messages, guidance, music, or tones that others cannot perceive. If you often talk to yourself and sometimes respond, you are likely connecting to the spiritual realm through your voice. It's much more common than you might think. This gift also shows itself if you hear your name whispered and there isn't anyone around. It may be discombobulating, but it is a message to explore this gift.

Clairsentience: Also known as "clear feeling," clairsentience involves the ability to sense or feel energy, emotions, or physical sensations from people, places, or objects. Clairsentients may pick up on the emotions or vibrations of others without any direct communication. Empaths sit in this area, often uncomfortably, when they do not know how to be in control of how much information they take in or how to let it bounce off or pass right through. It can get stuck and make you feel heavy from others' emotions. But remember, you are in control. Unregulated empathic gifts feel like a curse to those who do not know how to manage them and turn them into a superpower.

Claircognizance: This is the ability to know things without any logical explanation or prior knowledge, called "clear knowing." Claircognizant individuals may receive sudden insights, knowledge, or understanding about a situation or person. If you've ever known something was going to happen and then it did, you likely felt a rush of fear for how that was possible. If that fear stays present and you do not process it, it will most likely be blocked the next time. You may not have shared this with many people, as you didn't know if they would believe you. That is a widespread trait of those with this gift. They keep it to themselves, thinking they are a bit crazy. If you have this gift turned on and activated, you learn to pay attention to everything you know and track it to see the results and why you got the message in the first place.

Telepathy: This is the ability to transmit or receive thoughts, feelings, or information from one mind to another without using the usual senses or verbal communication. Telepathic communication can occur between individuals and even over long distances. This is an interesting gift I see with many people, yet they often don't know what is happening. If you can easily complete someone's sentences, hear the words, or know the thoughts they didn't speak, you are likely connecting through telepathy. It's a wild and wonderful experience, and it's more common than you might think.

Psychometry: Psychometry is the ability to receive information or impressions about a person, object, or place through touch. Psychometrists may perceive past events, emotions, or experiences associated with the object or person they are in contact with.

Mediumship: Mediumship is the ability to communicate with spirits, guides, or entities from the spiritual realm. Mediums communicate with dead people. Mediums may receive messages, guidance, or evidence from deceased loved ones or other spiritual beings. Many people shy away from mediumship, as they think of how Hollywood has presented it—people constantly being followed by ghosts. That couldn't be further from the truth. Through my years of experience, I believe many people receive messages from people who have passed on, and they classify them as from other sources. This is OK; the messages can be received, and you can classify them in any way that makes you feel comfortable.

In the North, we will focus on clairsentience (clear feeling) and claircognizance (clear knowing). These are the baseline of inherent intuition every human has experienced at some stage in their life. Clear knowing and clear feeling are more developed forms of intuition. All "clairs" sit in the North, as they come through the body offering clarity, and each one can be charted on the elemental wheel of seeking sacred magic.

Clear knowing and clear feeling are often confused. How you classify what you know or feel to be true makes no difference. This means you may not know the difference between what you "know" and what you "feel." Defining it specifically matters less than learning how to trust it and how to develop it and remembering it will likely come with a hint of other gifts. Call it what you want, but I will call it your psychic gifts.

Here are the three most important areas to focus on while sitting in the North when you want to activate your psychic gifts.

First and foremost, the key to awakening your gifts lies in knowing and connecting with your body. This is not a mere suggestion but a crucial step I've emphasized in this book. It's crucial in understanding energy and magic, and it's the most important step in activating your psychic gifts. The yes/no ritual you did earlier is just the starting place. There are more in-depth rituals in the ritual section in Part Two. These rituals are designed to help you understand your body's signals when distinguishing between a yes and a no. They also encourage you to practice deep feeling and knowing exercises in your daily life.

Second, write it down—anything you feel or know, even if it makes no sense at the time. Remember, you won't always get it right when you begin, and tracking it is the only way to know. Use the notes app on your phone or carry a journal to list things you know or feel, even if you don't know why or how. When you track it, you'll see a pattern of what is happening. There is enormous power that comes from giving yourself "proof" of your power. If you don't write it down, you may forget or not be able to connect the dots as easily.

Third, in order to feel the deep connection to all things in nature and in the unseen worlds, we must disconnect from the sources that take us away from them—phones, constant stimulation, noise, mainstream media, all of it. We live in a time where distraction is the prime goal for many people's lives. You may not even realize that your spare time is so filled with other things that there isn't any space for connection to the spiritual realm. Begin the digital detox I've outlined for you in the rituals section. This will amplify everything you do to truly awaken your psychic gifts.

We are conditioned to be in a constant state of digital stimulation, and we have to intentionally choose to schedule periods without it. Not only is this imperative to developing our spiritual and psychic gifts, but it's also imperative for our health. Our body needs time to recenter and recharge, and our nervous system needs to do its magic to regulate. It's choosing to live a more meaningful and healthy life and the key to opening up your psychic gifts. This is sacred magic.

If you conduct spells, do rituals, or even meditate, you know these are powerful practices to manipulate energy and create change. But if you jump right back into your phone and the digital stimulation after a ritual or spell, you will miss the portals you open and the spiritual guidance that is always ripe for you to pick. For the love of all that is holy, stay with your rituals and spells for much longer than you think necessary before turning your phone or computer back on.

Imagine doing a powerful ritual to connect with the energy of your intuition. You've cleared your field, worked plant magic, and shifted your body to be open to receiving messages and feeling light and clear. You've worked hard to connect to your body and have brought in answers to the questions you were asking. Your body is lit up with knowledge and connection, then, bam, you open Instagram and see an ad for how to lose weight. Your mind will say, "See, I told you your body is out of shape, and this is the sign to change it," which rips us right out of the connection to our body and puts us in a place to buy more stuff. You'll lose your aligned state and go back to trying to be something different. That ad isn't a sign—it is a sales tactic to make you buy another thing you don't need. Companies do that by showing you what you lack and where you are not perfect. And all the work you did in the ritual will be erased with the old programming about yourself. The initial messages you received will be drowned out if you jump right into digital noise. Don't do it!

When you embark on the magical journey of learning to disconnect from the digital world and reconnect with your inner world, there is no going back. You'll see the current matrix of our time and how it is the biggest block to remembering the magic inside us. Go slow and practice daily. Write out reminders on sticky notes about connecting to your body and listening and knowing. Keep the yes/no body ritual nearby and do it regularly, spend time in nature, and ground daily. Then you'll see this new way I'm teaching you to find yourself, and your magic will start to feel like the most natural thing in your life.

Contemplation questions

For each of these questions, you can follow up with describing the event as it relates to psychic gifts.

1. When was a time that I knew something to be true but denied it?

2. When was a time I shared something I knew (might call it intuition) with someone else and they didn't listen?

3. Have I ever listened to something or felt something so deeply yet had no way to track that it was actually true?

4. Have I ever heard my name called when nobody was around?

5. Have I ever seen movement in my peripheral vision?

6. When did I last think of someone and they called shortly after or I thought of a song and it played?

Chapter Ten
The Spirits

To explore the North spirits, you will need to set aside your beliefs about spirits, ghosts, and things that go bump in the night for a few moments. I'll ask you to continue to be undefined and open while we go into this realm of spirits. I'll weave magic for you by sharing a wild story that might make you wonder if this is reality or if I've gone way off into the deep end. The answer is both—it was real and I was in the deep end. The deep end is where the spirit world opens up our senses to what is unseen in our daily lives.

In the fall of 2021 I was deep into planning WitchFest, the largest event I had ever planned. While planning and preparing, I spent much of my time meditating and going into journey spaces that allowed me to see how the event was to unfold and what I needed to know, using my gifts to check in on my alignment. The event itself was huge and jam-packed with activities. It was one part market and fall activities and one part me with several other witches conducting rituals on stage for thousands of people.

For me to be taking rituals to the stage (the rituals I teach on the initiate path are a closed practice rooted in the Golden Dawn tradition, which is not available for public consumption anywhere online) was a new way of holding these ancient rituals. I knew it was time to bring them out of the underground hidden portals and into the light for others to feel and witness. To do so, I had a lot of my own layers of fear and conditioning to overcome, so I spent much time in meditation and journey space—to check in with my spirit and my soul to make sure this was the right path.

A journey is more than just a meditation; it's moving from one plane of existence to another after meditating. A slow meditation is meant to clear your mind and settle into the void of nothing in order to clear and release. A journey goes from the meditative state into another place, such as into a forest or beside a fire. It happens in your mind and is usually guided by someone to take you there and back out. It's a combination of a trance state and astral travel. I lead a lot of journeys for others, and because I'm a very experienced leader of these spaces, it's easy to take myself to other places without someone guiding me.

Prior to the big event I was preparing to lead, I led myself on many journeys that I thought would be more like meditation, but my spirit moved quickly into other realms.

Two months before the event, I entered into journeying; deeply breathing, I closed my eyes, counted down from ten, and went into the spiritual realm. In the first journey, I could feel the dampness against my skin and my vision was obscured by the fog and mud surrounding me. Voices were muted, color was unseeable, and my body felt heavy like lead. I was sinking to the bottom of a sinkhole. I was there immediately without any effort on my part to lead myself on a journey. This new journey place felt good, so I stayed, quietly relaxing into it and wondering what this place was. I stayed until I was ready to return to my body. I began slowly counting myself outward, took many deep breaths,

The Spirits

and returned to my body. I took a few more deep breaths and opened my eyes, wondering where I had just gone.

A few days later I entered into journey space again and found myself in a similar unknown place. It felt a little like the underworld I had journeyed to before but not quite the same. This new place felt comforting, even in the murky damp water I floated in.

For days this happened—I journeyed, found myself in this damp dark place that actually felt comfortable, and sank in and surrendered to this new place.

After several returns to this place, on one of the journeys, I relaxed a little deeper into this mystical realm. I began to notice more and could hear muted sounds all around me, but I wasn't able to decipher what they were. I relaxed even deeper until I felt comfortable enough to allow my inner sight to explore where I was. I looked around and an immediate electrical hit through my body startled me. I noticed there were twenty to thirty others in this place alongside me. I had not explored this place with my inner vision and was surprised to see there were others there, patiently waiting for me to find my vision in this mystical place. They were facing me with an intense energy I hadn't felt before in such a place. I realized we were underwater.

I could see above the waterline and the life happening above but underwater where we were it was quiet. And it wasn't typical water; this water felt thick and limited my freedom to roll around and play as water journeys normally are. And dark, it was so dark. The beings with me had long, dirty hair and their faces were of the human kind and were completely still and stoic. Their gaze never left my eyes the entire time. I felt hot under their gaze yet cold from the damp water we were in. Somehow, this nonphysical place I was traveling to in my mind that took my spirit with it also felt familiar.

There was no sound, no sharing of messages, and certainly no movement. Just their gaze. I closed my eyes in this spirit world I had found myself in and just rested. It was comforting there in the dark. I didn't know exactly why, but it was the solitude I needed in that moment.

Sacred Magic

I know the unsettled feeling I had was related to the energy and blessings I was planning to offer the dead while I was on stage.

I am comfortable going into the dark places where others see grief. I see working with the dead as an honoring of the continuation of a bloodline. I find comfort in communicating with the dead because they pass into a new form of light when their soul transitions out of their body. Their spirits feel like the greatest form of love we can experience—the love of our soul having returned home and looking back at those we love who are still on Earth living a human life. I recognize this is very different than how you may have been taught to view the dead.

Death was going to be in the air at WitchFest; that's how I planned it. That's the honoring and remembrance I wanted to see take place.

I continued to journey to this place. Rituals, deep breaths in and out. Day after day. I returned to the same place. About a month before the event, the beings that were with me were faced forward instead of facing me. Several of them had moved into an ancient warrior stance, legs bent, chests high.

I knew they had a message for me, but it wasn't quite there yet. I carried on with event planning and journeying when I had time. I spent a lot of time in solitude during this period, in part because the journeys were so powerful, but also because there was a weight on my shoulders about these rituals taking place on a stage for people to view.

On a later journey, the beings were there and no longer in their warrior stance but instead were circled up, and they let me float and hover in the center. I could feel the love. Waves of comfort pulsed through my body in a low hum of vibration. I definitely liked it here in this strange place where the outside world was gone.

I moved around the murky water, getting closer to the beings one-by-one. And then I spoke, in the way that you do in journeys when you are in water. I spoke with my thoughts and sent a question to them. I asked, *Why am I here and what is this place?*

The Spirits

They responded, also telepathically, sending thoughts into my mind: *We are the council, the ones that have come before you and have died for doing what you are about to do. We are protecting you from the forces that have once walked your plane, that destroy magic, and detest power being in the hands of women. We are protecting you by bringing you here with us to take refuge and prepare. It's safe here. We're with you, and you can stay as long as you like. This is the swamp.*

The swamp. That's what the magical place was.

I came out of the journey and went straight to the easel where a blank canvas sat waiting for fresh paint, and I began painting the swamp to process what was happening as I like to do. I wrote the experience on the canvas. I drew the faces I had seen and captured all the experiences I had there in a flurry of colors, then I painted over it in black like mud. Then more colors and then back to black.

I know it is wild to read this, and you may be thinking that this is beyond anything you have heard before, and trust me, I felt the same. Magic and wonder are a regular part of my life, but this experience was moving me, moment by moment. Each time I went in, I came out changed.

I continued into the final stretch of planning the event, all the while swirling between the swamp and the human world. I felt refuge, the love, and the quiet when I was in the swamp. I fell in love with this magical place, even though at times it felt heavy. It felt heavy because the outside stimulation during this time was so busy and full of details that the swamp was the complete opposite and forced me to let it all go. This was not an easy task with an event quickly approaching with massive numbers expected to attend.

Two weeks before the event, I journeyed back into the swamp. The council said telepathically, *It's time we show you what you can harvest here with us. It's time to come out of the swamp.* I was still centered among them in the back, and I witnessed them, one by one, walk out of the dark, murky, muddy dark water and sit on the edge where the land and swamp met. I stayed behind and allowed only my head out of the watery thickness. I saw them sitting next to this pool of murky water surrounded by lush greenery.

One week before the event—rituals, deep breaths, and back I went into the swamp. They said, *The swamp is the most fertile ground for anything to grow. Come sit with us and see for yourself.*

In this journey, I walked out and onto the edge where the land meets the swamp and sat with them—warriors and priestesses. I noticed some had the most intricate headdresses and markings on their bodies. They sat facing the swamp and let me sit among them. The moment I came and sat with them, tears streamed down my face, both in the journey and on my face in my human body.

I could see in a holographic-type shimmer, the wounds and harm that had been done to their bodies. They changed from the beings I had been with up until then to something different.

One by one, they changed. They became something scarred that reflected pain in their eyes. They shifted back and forth between these states. Wounds appeared on their bodies. And then, and then ... it dawned on me that I was seeing how they died.

I was seeing how they died when they were human. Rope burns were around their necks. Stab wounds appeared, some with blood running between thighs, and the ever-present fire off in the distance that I know was the cause of many of their deaths.

I stayed in the murky water and looked at these beings that had come and felt my body ache with a type of pain that lasts thousands of years. The type of pain that only the swamp can mute.

I left the journey that time utterly changed. I was enraged, sad, and very weepy. That was my last visit to the swamp.

The event was on track and the day came for us to open the hearts of the audience in complete initiation for those in attendance and for me to honor the dead in a public ritual. The day was a blur of activity and magic. High Priests and Priestesses were holding space for anyone who came to the table of witches to honor their loved ones and offering a rose petal to write their name on or a

The Spirits

bay leaf that would be burned in a central cauldron. There was joy and a little bit of fear regarding how many witches were in attendance.

I was circulating among the crowds, moving energy, and swaying to the rhythm of the spirits that were all around us. I could feel the connection to the dead that we were honoring. It was beautiful and moving. I watched people participate in the activities and shed tears of joy remembering their loved ones. I watched families bring their young children to the table of witches to write the names of those they loved.

I was in awe of witnessing people experience real witch work. They held their hearts out for us to heal. They held hands and wept together. And then my body moved deeper and deeper into trance states as we prepared for the main stage rituals that were to come.

I don't remember much of what happened after I stepped onto the stage. I was in my body and also in the spirit world honoring the dead. What I do know is that the council from the swamp was with me. They entered the space and entered my body the moment I stepped on stage.

I do remember that after I completed the honoring of the dead on stage, I felt my body start to shake. I remember the feeling, not the visuals around me or what was happening around me while still on stage. I have a flash of seeing the circle of priestess's eyes looking at me and someone saying, "It's time to go." I was no longer just me; I was "we." I was all the witches in the swamp inside one human body. I was them, and they were me.

I was told afterward by my sister witches that when they saw me shaking, they knew immediately that it was time to quickly wrap up the on-stage portion to ensure I was out of the public eye. The next thing I remember is a grumbling of pain, death, and anger that was coming out of the core of my body. The pain and anger inside of me wanted to come out, and I could feel myself pushing them out. I was pushing and moving and releasing. I had no other connection to where I was or who was there. I needed only to get it out. Waves of intense movement of energy from inside my body were rolling like waves of thunder. Inside me, in that exact place where the twinge had been for weeks, was a searing red-hot ball of pain that was consuming me.

I didn't realize that while I was expelling that pain, I had begun to scream and cry out loud with a guttural force that changed the fabric of time. I was releasing the council from the swamp and honoring their pain through my body. My earthly, human body had connected to each spirit in the swamp, and I was physically in the human, material world processing it.

The word for this is "keening," and I've since seen pictures of myself while keening, and my face is expressive of the anguish and death. I didn't know the word or that it was happening at the time nor had I ever experienced anything like it before. I was wailing out loud in the deepest of grief for those who had come before.

To this day, it was by far one of the greatest honors I have received from the spirit world. It was also a lot of big energy to process, and I still shudder slightly when I think of that feeling. It changed my soul's purpose to understanding how important this work is and how blessed I am to have chosen this time to come into human form and be the living embodiment of what it means to be a witch. It was a deeply profound experience to have this happen through my body. It changed me.

To this day, I have not watched any footage of the event; my memories are more powerful than any camera could capture. I need only to look at the painting I made to remember the feeling or just close my eyes and return to the swamp to remember.

We often neglect all aspects of what the North and the earth offer. The swamp was then and still is the place I go for the deepest levels of transformation by tapping into the fertile grounds of stillness, sight, and spirit allies. You are here in this moment in the North with the opportunity to step deeper into your truth and your own body. This time will provide clarity about your wisdom and your spiritual gifts.

You do not need to be engulfed in the swamp with witch spirits to tap into the fertile grounds the swamp can offer. But you can take yourself into nature

The Spirits

and connect to the earthbound spirits supporting you. Slowly, at your own pace, and with what feels right in your body.

This is why connection to your body is important to this work. You need to know what feels good to you and what doesn't feel good. Discernment about what type of spirits you want to allow comes from being connected to your body. Make no mistake that I allowed myself by choice to experience the swamp and the witches that were there. At any time, I could have said, "No, this isn't for me," and it would have stopped. Knowing more about me, you can see I'm comfortable going into the deep trenches that both humans and spirits have experienced. It's one of the gifts I carry close to my heart in this lifetime, my ability to go into dark places alongside others. That may not ever be something you wish to experience, and that is your choice. But for me, I choose to walk with the dead.

The North has a powerful elemental spirit of its own. The spirit of the North feels like a warm blanket on a cold day. The North feels like a gentle striptease of your soul until it's naked and raw. It's a blank slate when you want to begin again. It's where we go to let our old versions die so something new can be born like a tiny little plant that sprouts on a warm spring day.

The spirit of the North is a healer. I call her a she when it's the great womb of healing. I call him a he when it's the father god that is present in all rebirth that occurs, and he holds space as a steadfast masculine force while the mother opens her womb for the new. It's both and neither.

The spirit of the earth is the spirit of the element of earth. Trying to wrap your arms around this spirit is like trying to wrap your arms around the expansive size of a mountain. It's bigger than you can imagine. It's all things you need at any moment to create the space to go inward. To rest. To gain wisdom and understanding of the cycles of all things. The spirit of the North is everything in one directional spirit.

Take a moment to think of pictures of the Earth taken from satellites. You've seen at least one photo of this beautiful blue (water) planet that is full of life in its green and brown wonder (nature). That's how big the spirit of the North is.

Many additional spirits live in the North and call it home. They will all aid you in your quest for sacred magic and deeper connection to your life's purpose.

A few examples are the spirits of the lands, the shadow walkers, ancestors, faeries, and any human who once walked on the earth. These are the dwellers of the middle world and the underworld. They have not ascended into higher dimensional planes, which may be temporary, or they may be destined to stay earthbound. It is not for us to know the reason why so many spirits stay earthbound; it is an opportunity for us to learn from them, commune with them, and honor them. Doing so will bring great reward and blessings into your life.

Earth spirits are mainly those that dwell in the earthly plane or underneath the earthly plane. They have a direct tie to humans.

Air spirits are those that come from higher dimensions such as angels, archangels, and deities we call god.

Fire spirits are deities, gods, and goddesses that stand for change and deep layers of transformation. Fire spirits stand for change but can also come in with any elemental magic.

Water spirits are found in the earth's waters and in the rebirth process of any aspect of life. They can also come in with any elemental magic.

Many underworld spirits in the North also reside in the direction of the South and can be found in either direction, as the underworld represents fire, which we'll cover in the third book.

Higher dimensions and higher-dimensional beings aren't necessarily better. There are beings meant to support humans in all phases of our

The Spirits

experience, and some come from higher dimensions because they're the mind and thoughts. Some spirits stay in one dimension and some move on or change as the spirit progresses. Other cosmic beings (such as angels) are not earthbound spirits but are great and powerful allies. We'll discuss them in the second book, the East.

The North is the place of both the middle world and the underworld. Many people begin to feel a tinge of nervousness when I talk about the underworld. The easiest way I can alleviate that fear is to explain that the middle world (our human reality) is far scarier than any lower world or underworld. As humans, we create great harm to our planet and fight and kill each other, children, and animals, and we harm ourselves far more than any spirit from the underworld. We are the ones who create and live in destruction. I'm not referencing you (or me for that matter), but as a collective of humans, we are destructive.

The underworld is the place where we hide our deepest trauma, our pain, and our hidden parts. Spirits that lived in painful ways in human life can remain in the underworld. There are even spirits whose job it is to be a guiding light in the underworld, similar to the witches of the swamp. The swamp is a place to the North, with its murky, muddy waters, part earthly underworld and part water. I experienced the swamp as this type of underworld energy, especially as I saw the painful ways the witches had died. The underworld is also inside all of us as a place we go when we want to heal and clear patterns and beliefs once and for all. It is also a place we are swept into when in the throes of pain, whether we know it or not.

At the most basic level of any spiritual path, experiencing the energy of the spirit for the direction of the North is life changing. It does not matter if you know the spirits are underworld spirits, middle world spirits, or upper world spirits; it only matters how interacting with the spirit feels to you.

At this stage on our journey with the North, you have a strong understanding of the elements, the connection to our body, the cycle of death/rebirth, and the inward nature of the North. You know how to root down deep into the earth and gather energy and how to root down deep to let go of energy. You know the North is the place to go for rest and contemplation.

We can call on the spirit of the North as part of the cycle we live each day by detoxing from our addiction to social media and putting our feet on the earth.

We can call on the spirit of the North as part of the cycle we live each week when we tend to the devotion of our homes and altars.

We can call on the spirit of the North as part of each moon cycle when we allow our body time to rest and create our manifestations from that rested place.

We can call on the spirit of the North as part of the cycle we live each year in recognizing each time we've returned to the North and let it support our quest for surrendering into deeper levels of truth.

The spirit of the North is ever present; even when we don't recognize it, it's there. This is because it comes from and through nature itself, and nature on this planet is all around us and does not cease to exist even when it changes form.

There are cycles in each cycle. There are spirals in each cycle. There are patterns in each spiral that can tell us where we are at any time. Taking one spiral or cycle out at a time and knowing what it feels like and how to navigate it, we can call upon what is needed to put us in direct flow with the rhythm of the universe.

To connect to the spirit of the North is to connect to the spirit of the earth, vibrationally, in its various forms. I work with the North in the darkest of times when doing healing work for students who are working through trauma. I am in the North when I show up in the spirit world as a shadow walker and do cord cuttings for others. I work in the North when I'm processing my own fears and when I need to birth something now. I allow myself to sink deeply into the North when I know I need to replenish and create.

Read this and let it flow through you. Write your own if you so wish but creating a reminder of the "feeling" of the earth spirit to the North is a powerful yet simple way to be reminded of the power of the North. The most powerful

The Spirits

way to continue the evolution of your relationship with the spirit of the North is to keep a connection to nature and to your body.

In the heart of the Northern winds, where whispers of ancient tales weave through the frost-kissed air, lies the spirit of the North, a silent thread that connects all things. In its silent expanse, where the icy tendrils of winter reach out to touch the farthest corners of the world, where the sun shines and shimmers on the ocean, and the rain falls in the desert, there exists a profound harmony that binds me to it all. It is here, amid the snow-laden forests and the shimmering auroras, that I feel the primordial language of the earth speaking to me—a long-lost language of the secrets of creation itself.

In the embrace of the earth's ancient text, I find solace and sanctuary. For the land beneath my feet is not merely soil and stone but a living, breathing entity infused with the wisdom of eons past. It whispers to me of the cyclical nature of existence, of the eternal dance of birth, death, and rebirth. Like the roots of the mightiest trees, I am anchored to this sacred soil, drawing sustenance from its depths and finding nourishment in its enduring embrace. And as I wander through the labyrinthine pathways of life, I am reminded that I am never truly alone, for I am held deeply by the earth itself, cradled in the arms of a timeless spirit that knows no bounds. Thank you, spirit of the North. And so it is.

We will now explore some specific spirits of the North, such as land spirits and ancestors.

LAND SPIRITS

When you think of the thousands of years humans have been walking this planet, you might also consider how these humans were buried and how their energy can remain long after they are alive. Billions of bodies have been buried on the grounds we all live on. It's likely we walk on top of old graves or soil that has grown in combination with ashes and remains of bodies.

Most land spirits have once lived as humans on the lands we call home. Even though we may have torn down the vegetation and scraped nature away to make more room to build houses and businesses, the energies of those previous humans remain. This means land spirits are roaming around no matter where you reside. The question is whether you know how to connect to them. Working with land spirits where you live can completely change how your family makes its home. Whether it's a room you rent in a tall high-rise in the middle of a city, a cabin far into the woods, or, like me, a home (I call it a witch castle) on a remote island, they all have spirits you can work with to create a deeper connection to the earth and to the spaces you create. Regardless of how you live, land spirits are there and can either work in your favor or against you.

I crafted a spell for one of my students, a litigation lawyer, who had an important case coming up that was meaningful for her. She was protecting a family who had been harmed by a company's negligence. She asked for spell work to move the case in her favor.

I gave her many steps to sway the outcome, knowing that many people are involved in legal cases and the spell work is multifaceted. Lawyers for both sides, the company's owners, and the responsible parties all had a vested interest and would be energetically working against any spell I created; even if it was just a job they performed, they still had an intention of "winning" and my client "losing." The most important part of the ritual I asked her to complete was to connect with the spirits of the lands at the courthouse. They were powerful allies in supporting justice and would aid in the outcome. The ritual included collecting dirt from the courthouse property (safely without

The Spirits

breaking any laws, especially on courthouse property) and leaving offerings behind. Then she returned home with the dirt and continued connecting to the spirits from her own home.

These powerful rituals and spells not only turned this case in her favor, but it also came out better than they had hoped. This is 100 percent the result of working with land spirits.

The easiest and often eye-opening way to work with spirits of the lands is to start thinking about the fact that you live on lands that were likely once tribal lands. Those lands were taken away from them and many dwellings were likely built on the lands. Think beyond the 1900s, think beyond the dirt and construction, and think of those who might have lived there before houses (as we know them today) were a thing. Maybe they had babies or raised their families there, or likely they had their lands stolen and had people they loved killed for the land. People might have used your location as a pass-through to get supplies or create camps and communities. The list of possibilities is endless.

I often see land spirits come into a human's life when the humans do not take care of the land the way the spirit wants. Yes, you are in control in the human realm, but if you purchase a property where many farmers once lived, they might have something to say if you decide to make significant changes. If the land spirits desire to see part of the land remain wild and you continue to chop down trees for expanding housing or to put in a pool, they (might) revolt. I'm not saying you shouldn't do the things you want to do on your land—you can and should. I'm saying to commune with the spirits first for their blessing. Tell them your wishes and how your family (and you) will enjoy the space. Tell them it's OK and honor them with offerings. Most of the time any disharmony with the lands will become smooth afterward. This doesn't happen to everyone, as most land spirits have many other experiences of people invading what was once theirs, but I see it enough with clients and students that I know there are still relational ways that land spirits desire to be honored.

Start in contemplation of where you live, why, and how you feel on the lands where you reside. Then research what tribes once occupied the place you call home. There are many sites online you can use to research native tribes and the history of where you live. This research will give you valuable insight into what types of land spirits you can connect with.

Fair warning: Once you open this door and allow them in, you should expect a much deeper connection to your location and more blessings to come your way. You should expect a new type of spirit ally to enter into your field that will greatly transform how you experience the spirit world. And it is magical. They will aid your quest for wholeness and your soul's purpose and may even become an integral part of how you experience magic, not to mention they will become powerful protectors of your home. I provide an overview of rituals to connect with land spirits in Part Two.

Ancestors

Like land spirits, many of our ancestors stay close by and reside in the realm of the North. Although ancestors can be accessed in each direction because they are connected through our bloodline and our body, the most powerful way to connect with them is in the North part of the spiral path.

We may or may not know our ancestors, and both known and unknown ancestors want to see you live a deeply successful life. They do not want to see any unhealthy patterns they may have passed down be carried on. They see the highest version of you and can be the greatest mystical cheerleader you can have in your spirit posse. They are always with you.

One of the most important lessons I learned early on while doing readings and using my seer vision to help others gain clarity is that, like it or not, we've been given certain beliefs through conditioning from our parents, who were conditioned by their parents, and we carry it forward and condition our children. We can't escape it; it's like the operating system we carry was imprinted on us at birth. Recognizing this is fundamental work to healing your patterns and choosing to live another way. The heaven on earth way. It requires you to see through to the roots that created these patterns in your family line.

All of you alive at this time and reading this book have had grandparents or great-grandparents who lived during the Second World War, which was a time when scarcity, primarily around food, money, and safety, was real. Scarcity as a whole was their life, and everything was tight.

This is to say that the patterns you carry in your life around money, your lack of relationship with it, or how you see yourself in this lifetime all go back to the lens through which your parents were created, which then created you.

When my grandmother passed away, I received the original journal of my grandfather from his time in World War II. From enlisting and training to serving and experiencing his first live combat, it was all there written in his hand. I discovered that he had received several Bronze Stars for valor, but my family had no idea. Reading through his words at what he experienced in his twenties was one of the greatest gifts I've ever received. This taught me about the man who raised my father, which created the beliefs and principles that conditioned my father, who in turn influenced me. I understood more about my father, and in doing so, I understood more about myself and my beliefs.

The power of this knowledge lets you sit with it and determine if it's to be a part of your sacred magic or not. Knowing your ancestors is knowing yourself and how you came to feel and believe the things that you do, giving you the choice to decide what to carry moving forward.

Working with our ancestors is more than just a ritual we do to invoke the power of their support; it's a deep dive into our own roots to see ourselves more clearly and understand what led us to this exact moment in time. It's knowledge and knowledge leads to being able to make more powerful and aligned choices. It's a power move toward a magical life to begin to understand why your parents are the way they are. That knowledge will help you understand why you are the way you are. You gain power through this knowledge when you remember that you can choose what you want to be and what you want to experience. You can and do get to choose to stay the same and carry old patterns or to change.

Many spiritual and witch teachers hold the belief that when we heal ourselves, we are also healing seven generations behind us and seven generations in front of us. We can go through the time-weaving process and rewrite what we've experienced by changing the lens through which we view the experience itself. To change the lens and rewrite the story, we first need to know where we come from—the good, the bad, the magical, and the traumatic, and then turn it all into a neutral energy and see what lies ahead. This is why I asked at the beginning and several times through this book for you to remain undefined. Being undefined means to return to neutrality and become completely reprogrammable. The spiral path is accepting that you can and *are* doing your own programming by what you choose. Not choosing is also a choice.

When we approach our ancestors, we do so for two reasons: Number one is to bring in these powerful allies, and number two is to heal any parts of our lineage currently impacting us. This is where the "c" of choice between the "b" of birth and "d" of death comes into play. What part of your lineage do you want to carry forth? And what part do you want to heal and not see carried forward in generations after you?

I worked for a year one-on-one with a beautiful human who had a grandparent who was a violent criminal. My client's grandfather served time and died in prison. His daughter (my client's mother) had a long history of trying to avoid anything spiritual, as she didn't want the spirit of her father in anyone's life. She was afraid of carrying even one gene of her father. The mother lived a very successful life and raised three children. She was a strict parent and attended church every Sunday, and my client attended with her.

The client came to me, as he felt a deep calling to explore his ancestors and do work in the spiritual realm. You see, he was a medium and had been seeing spirits since he was a child. Yet he never had anyone to speak to about it because, when he was a child, his mother forcefully shut it down and taught him how evil it was. When we began to explore his history and beliefs about mediumship, we tracked the root of this fear to the fear his mother carried about her violent father. My client knew of this family history, but it was never discussed in detail, only explained as to why he didn't see his maternal grandparents. He was told they were bad people. His mother had cut all connections to her family many years earlier.

As we dove deeper and deeper into his ancestral work, I connected to the spirit of his grandfather several times in deep ritual space. Through me, he shared with his grandson a powerful vision of himself sitting on a tree stump and crying. My client's grandfather's spirit showed me his remorse through his tears and body language while sitting on that stump, and I felt his remorse in my body. I passed this spirit's message on to his grandson, who himself had seen the same vision many times but didn't know who it was. This vision had come to him in dreamtime, and when I described it, all the pieces fell into place. He had been hearing from his grandfather in his dreams.

In my client's case, his mother was still alive while he was doing this work, and slowly, ever so slowly, he was able to open the lines of communication and talk to his mother about what it was like being that man's child and the fear she carried. It is not always possible to walk the truths and clear the lineage with our parents or grandparents, but it will clear their souls' imprints when we do this work, even just for ourselves.

His and my work together was focused on going to the spiritual realm and developing his gifts. He knew that for him to fully face and release the wounding his mother had passed onto him, he would need to talk to his mother and go deeper into the wounding. He said he felt he was also meant to open the doors for healing for his mother. He attended traditional therapy at the same time as doing the spiritual work, and he developed the tools to also work with his mother.

When our work was completed, he had made many baby steps forward with his mother, who had accepted his gifts, and although she may never want to commune with her father in spirit form, she loved her son enough to understand that her fears had become his fears. That was not something she had wished upon her son by choice. It was an old trauma and was her own fear.

This client is currently a practicing medium, and his gifts are fully awake and online. Through his mediumship, he uses his gifts to help clear others of generational trauma.

In many cases, we do not have human-to-human access to our parents or grandparents. That doesn't make this work any less powerful, as their spirit is accessible. They still reside with us, even in the form of a simple orb of light.

In Part Two, I will provide rituals and workings to connect to your ancestors. Your life will change more magically than your mind can imagine. You can clear past patterns and beliefs in your lineage by working on them to improve your life and find the truths you carry. These are all steps in finding sacred magic.

The Spirits

Contemplation questions

1. Have I ever felt my ancestors give me a message? How did I know it was them?

2. When did I suspect a spirit or otherworldly being was in my field?

3. Have things in my house randomly moved when nobody was around? What did I tell myself about it at the time?

4. What fears do I have about interacting with spirits that are nonhuman?

5. What spirits do I want to communicate with?

6. Why do I want to (or not want to) communicate with spirits?

Chapter Eleven
Journeying

Journeying across the veil and into the spiritual plane, which I've spoken of often so far, is a core practice I teach and live by. It's a way to bypass time and space and go deeper into mystical places where your human mind can be slowly quieted to experience the expansiveness of your soul. It's a magic-lined path of experiencing sacred magic that you can do at any time and any place. All you need to do to enter journey space is breathe, relax, and close your eyes.

There is one journey that changed my life. I've experienced it only one time, yet that one time forever changed my life.

During my first initiate path as a High Priestess years ago, one of the teachers led a journey that took us to the steps of an ancient temple. It was a guided meditation that swirled into a magical trance state that journeys can provide.

Sacred Magic

If meditation is a process of stilling the mind and body, a journey is a process of stilling the mind and body then moving to another place. In journeys, we intentionally move through the worlds and go someplace else, either natural or mystical. The place you go to is usually chosen by the person leading the journey to provide you with the framework of the destination, but you have the opening to move from there into further places of your own. This journey led us through an outdoor landscape and into a place where we ended up on the stairs of an ancient structure. All good journeys leave you with a choice to go further or stay where they left you.

Of course, I'm always all in for experiencing magic, and I walked up the steps and into the temple that looked like something from ancient Rome or Greece. It was old and a type of small stadium with rafters and tiers overlooking the main section.

When I walked in, it was quiet. Several beings were sitting at a table in the center of the stadium. They sat still and looked directly at me. They asked from across the room if I was ready. I didn't know what was happening, but I had surrendered and knew I had been guided here for a reason. I said yes to their question; yes, I was ready.

As I began to walk across the stadium floor toward the table, I glanced up and saw many stories of balconies that were filled with other beings that appeared as humans. I knew instantly that they were beings that had lived in another time. They were quiet and were all focused on me. I felt their gaze and their presence. I didn't feel nervous, nor did I wonder why everyone was looking at me. In my waking life, I often experience people looking at me or following me. I know my energy can be felt, and it draws people in. But their gaze felt different. Their eyes bore the look of what I can describe only as the feeling of liberation. The beings felt like liberated humans.

I got closer to the table and realized a long scroll was unwound on the table with a fountain pen next to it. There were others sitting at the table who spoke. "It is time for you to remember what you came for. It's time to sign. Are you ready?" I asked them who they were, and they said they were the warrior council and I was to be their leader. They said they had been waiting for a long time for this moment, and it was time.

In that moment, I felt the weight of what was being asked of me, even while in journey space. It felt familiar to me, the call to lead. I had always known this to be true on some level in my body. Although I was not surprised, the intensity of their gaze and the watchful eyes of everyone in the stadium brought a buzzy, electrical pulse through my body while on the journey. I knew this was a turning point in my life, even in the altered, trance-like state. I knew it in my real flesh and bone human body. The buzzing I felt has always been a sign I "feel" when I know what's happening will have a major impact.

I sat down and soaked in the quiet of the large space and somehow used my finger to sign my name on the scroll. My finger signed my name in red.

Suddenly, the entire stadium began chanting my name, and those sitting at the table said loudly, "It is done."

There was a deafening in my ears, and I was immediately thrust out of the journey. It isn't normal to jump right out of a journey. A slow return, coming out the way you go, is the safest way to travel to other realms. In this case, I jolted up like a lightning bolt and realized that I was in my bed at home. I had no idea how I had gotten there. I wondered if I had dreamed the entire thing. But that couldn't be; I had been in the temple with a teacher and other students. I wondered if during the journey, I had somehow lost time. I was very disoriented.

I determined that somehow after the journey the day before in my teacher's sanctuary, more than an hour from my home, I had returned home, but I had no idea how. I remembered the beginning and being on the journey but not the time in between. I did not remember returning home or getting into bed and falling asleep. It seemed like time had gone by, and I had not left the journey.

I spoke to my fellow students who were in the class with me at the time, and they affirmed that yes, we had journeyed, and yes, I had come out and left as usual. They said I was quiet but otherwise my normal self. They expressed wonder and excitement when I shared what had occurred, although to me it felt like I had lost a day.

I had zero recollection of anything after the journey itself, which means I drove home and put myself to bed without returning fully to my body. This is something I would never suggest you do, and when I lead journeys, I am always cautious to make sure people have fully returned to their body before they depart.

As I continued to process what had occurred, I knew I needed to draw the outline of what I had seen in the stadium in my journal. Over coffee the next day, I wrote it all out. I drew the stadium, the beings, and the experience. I still felt the words of those who spoke and the eyes of those who watched from above.

When I finished writing and drawing, I began my day slightly woozy and still trying to understand what had occurred. Later that morning when I went into my kitchen to start my morning rituals, I felt a sting on the pointer finger on my right hand. I looked down and saw a cut on my finger the size of a paper cut.

I stopped in my tracks and knew I had provided my signature in blood while in the spirit world, and the wound was fresh on my skin. I had gone into the journey to experience the nonmaterial world and bring change into my material world, forever changing the course of my life.

Of all the many initiations, journeys, and classes I've taken, this one created the most significant change in my life.

I had given my blood, my commitment, my holy yes, that I was ready. And within two years, I took up the mantle of temple keeper and opened a mystery school that now serves thousands of students a year on their path to remembering the magic they hold within them.

As with the sacred art of allowing yourself to surrender fully, whether it's in meditation or breathwork, creating a space for journeys is about creating a

JOURNEYING

sanctuary that provides the energy of surrender. The sanctuary I'm speaking of isn't just the physical space around you (that does matter); it's also about the sanctuary you have inside you to trust the process and surrender.

If the idea of journeying to other realms of time is new to you, it's OK; take it slow and work at a pace that feels good to you. You can begin the process of journeying to other worlds slowly and proceed as you become more comfortable. It will feel a little like dreaming while you are still awake.

This is one of the times to remain undefined, to put what you think you know to the side, and open yourself to the possibility that real magic exists. Real magic can be experienced in journey space when you move from one reality to the next. Sounds wild, right? Yet, it is not so far from the same experience you have during a guided meditation where you are led through a visualization process of leaving and returning to your body. It creates real opportunities to go into other realms to create what you desire and bring it back into your real, tangible human life.

I've taken people on journeys where they experienced, in very lifelike ways, their past lives. I've taken people on a journey of time to discover something critical they wished to know about the future. I've guided souls to the underworld to see what they were hiding in their shadows and bring it to the light to be cleared. And everything in between. I've never *not* been able to take someone into a visual experience where they witnessed the possibilities of other worlds.

If you've made it this far in the North, you know that magic is waiting for you here in the sacred place we find ourselves. Keep going and allow the journey experience that I'm about to share, to set into motion everything you've taken in so far.

First, you need to set up your space for the journey.

The best way to set up the physical space for journeys is to think comfort, such as pillows, soft blankets, or a chair for sitting up. When first learning to journey, find a quiet place without distractions.

Although you can journey in any setting or location, it's best to start with intentional space until you are comfortable going in and out before you do it on the fly in any random place. I can do short journeys when I have a moment and want information quickly, such as the doctor's office. When I have a long wait, I take myself on a journey into the spirit world to gain knowledge about my body while I'm waiting. I then have more significant questions and clarity of what I'm discussing with the doctor. If I arrive to a meeting or social event early, I'll stay in my car and do a short journey to prime myself for what is to come, again looking for insight and connection to the energy of the spirit world.

When I make short journeys, it's like tapping into my psychic gifts but a little different, as I allow myself the perspective that is not of this time and space and not of just my body. I can do this only because I have years of experience. You'll get there one day too.

You may wish to set up a special table or altar of items to prepare for your journey. Adding a journey altar is more about creating comfort in your environment to surrender and having a few items close by. A few items you may wish to bring to journey space are candles, water, and a journal. I also love to lie down for journeys, usually on the floor, so pillows are my favorite addition. I keep them stacked in most rooms so it's easy to sink in and surrender when I have a moment to do so.

If you have a tendency to fall asleep when you are reclined, it's best to use a chair and sit upright.

Whether you are on a specific quest for increased access to the spiritual plane want to experience real magic by working in an altered state (similar to a trance), or desire to experience more of the magic that lives in the spiritual realm, we'll go there together in a journey made for you.

A Journey for You

It's time to step away from our busy lives for a moment to experience the North in all its forgotten wisdom and to begin weaving our way deeper into ourselves. It's time for you to go on your own journey.

To experience this journey to the fullest, you should read it all the way through, then close the book and take yourself to this place. For the audio version where I lead you on this journey, visit Tahverlee.com/northresources. Having a voice to lead you is more powerful, but with practice and reviewing what is to take place, you can set yourself up to experience this journey to the fullest. I also record and provide new journeys on my YouTube channel and in many, many classes. There is a list in Part Three of this book of all additional resources.

Journeys involve using breathwork to slow down your system. Then we move into a relaxed state. I will provide the visual cues of the journey and include when to take a sacred pause and remain in the moment. From there, I will lead you back out.

Allow yourself at least thirty minutes to journey. Stay as long as you like, and when you come back out, note in your journal everything you experience. It all matters. Even if you don't know the meaning at the time, writing it down allows you to trace the sacred thread of knowledge in the future when it's time to revisit.

You cannot do a journey in a right or wrong way. You can experience it only to the level you are willing to surrender to the unknown and wild places within you.

Start by finding a comfortable position, either sitting or lying down. Do five deep breaths, ten counts in and ten counts out. Ever so slowly, feel the tension of the day leave your body and feel yourself relax deeper and deeper. Continue breathing in and out until you feel your body relax so deeply that you feel like sleep is just around the corner, but the goal is not to sleep. It's to stay in the liminal space between waking and sleeping.

Picture yourself lying on the softest green grass. Feel the damp, cool earth underneath your body and the warm sun off in the distance getting ready to set. You hear birds chirping, and a slight breeze tickles your skin. It feels so peaceful and quiet and warm. Your body is resting, and when you take a deep breath to soak it all in, you smell the grass and the fragrant flowers that must be somewhere nearby. You stay here and enjoy the sun until you feel it beginning to move behind the mountains off in the distance.

You sit up and look around and notice off to the right is a beautiful forest of trees, and you decide to go for a walk and visit them. You walk along the green grass, feeling the softness and dampness of earth. You continue walking until you come to the edge of the forest, and then you step into the forest, feeling surprised at how soft the dirt and leaves are under your feet. You reach out and touch a few of the trees as you continue to walk in the forest.

You feel the sun continuing to set, and although the forest is darkening, you have no problem seeing in front of you. You notice a faint glow up ahead, and you make your way closer and closer to this glow. You realize that it is a light that appears to be shining up from the ground. As you reach the edge of this hole, you see that it is a place where a tree once stood, and the tree has fallen and revealed an opening.

It's as if this opening and light have been created for you, and you decide to enter the opening in the earth. You use the old roots of the tree as a ladder and gently lower yourself down and enter into a tunnel that appears to be lit up by something at the end. You walk along the tunnel, hearing the sound of water running in the distance. You see other tree roots around you in the tunnel, almost as if they are moving aside to welcome you as you go. You get closer to the light source and come upon an opening into a large underground cave.

Journeying

It's the most beautiful place you have ever seen. There are trees growing with flowers of colors you have never seen before. It appears like they are sparkling. You see a waterfall off in the distance and continue to look around in amazement at the most lush, magical lands you have ever seen. The ground is covered in soft moss, and gigantic stones of crystals are everywhere. You see the sparkle of the stones is so bright that it has lit up this entire cave; this was the light that drew you here. Your gaze settles up ahead on a tree. The biggest tree of the cave. It has flowers of every color, shape, and size. It takes your breath away. You walk closer and closer and notice there is a small stool placed next to the trunk of this tree, and you take a seat. You pause here and take a rest. You feel the tree begin to speak to you in whispers.

(Pause here on the journey and stay as long as you like.)

What seems like hours later the tree slowly stops its enchanting whispers and with a final parting sentence says, "Take these with you and plant them in your own garden." You look down, and your hand all of a sudden is filled with seeds that look like tiny rainbows sparkling in your palm. You stand up and put these seeds in your pocket and turn around and place a hand on this magical tree and whisper "thank you."

You turn and head back to the tunnel knowing that it is now time for you to return. With one last glance over your shoulder, you begin to walk back through the tunnel. As you get closer to the opening in the earth under the tree, you see light coming now from the outside, and you use the roots to climb back up, and you notice the sun has risen again, and you have spent the night in the magical cave.

You return to the edge of the forest where you entered, and you find your place back on the grass and lie back down, feeling the sun's warmth on your face once again.

Return to the here and now. As you come out of the journey, it's important that you move your body, stretch, and clap loudly three times to make sure you have returned.

Grab your journal and note everything:

1. What did you see from the start to the end?
2. What did you feel?
3. How clearly were the sounds?
4. How did you feel entering the tunnel? Could you see the light and the fallen tree?
5. What appeared in the magical cave?
6. Describe it all and feel free to draw out anything you saw.
7. Be sure and take time to feel into any messages you received from the tree. It may take more time for you to fully understand what the tree was telling you, so write it all down and give yourself time to process.

Regardless of how you experienced this journey, through the written word or the audio version, let it be exactly the magic you needed in that moment. You can use the steps to slow your breath, to still your body and mind, and take yourself to any destination you desire. Allow yourself to experience each journey however it comes for you. There is no right or wrong way to journey; there's only doing it or not. Our busy lives and overstimulated minds can take time for us to step out of the mundane and into the spiritual realms. If you want to experience more of the realms that journeys take you to, keep practicing. Spend a few minutes a day stilling your breath and closing your eyes and letting your mind wander. Spend an hour each week taking yourself on your own journey or find a guided one to lead you.

Contemplation questions

1. Do I want to spend more time in the unseen worlds? Why?

2. I have fear about the unseen worlds because?

3. I struggle to make time for this in my day-to-day life because?

4. I want more magic in my life, and to experience it, I am willing to?

5. If I could choose one time in the future or past to visit in journey space, it would be?

Part Two
Rituals and Spells

Chapter Twelve
How to Get Started with Rituals and Spells

*I*T'S TIME TO PUT WHAT YOU'VE LEARNED so far into motion by practicing and bringing the knowledge of the North into your life. When you combine the knowledge of how magic works with the desire to live more freely, entire new paths in your life will open up and reveal what your soul is craving. To study magic is to study intentional transformation. The study helps you find where you are on the spiral path of life and turn it into a sacred magical stopping point. You'll sit for a while and shed old layers and make space for new ways of being to emerge.

The true power of everything I've shared so far can be known only by trying it and putting it into practice for yourself. To see it, feel it, and experience it within your own body. Knowledge is only one piece on the sacred magic path; the second piece is knowing for yourself how it feels, how it changes you as you work each ritual.

This is the time to allow yourself to remain undefined a little longer, staying open to change and growth. Sit in the void of not knowing who you can become and dwell awhile in the new place of possibilities.

My role in teaching you what is possible is coming to an end, but the journey of finding magic and what is most sacred to you is far from over. The next steps are for you to experience yourself and awaken the mysteries, spirits, and connections to what your heart and soul truly desire. The desire you seek lives inside of you, just waiting to be awakened. I can explain the possibilities, share my own magical ceremonies and magic, and even provide you with specific rituals and spells. However, it is your choice to try them and begin integrating them into your life. This awakening happens when you experience it in your body, a practice of finding and experiencing your power.

Let's talk for a moment about the difference between a ritual and a spell and why it matters to understand the distinction. A ritual is a set of actions, often ceremonial and performed according to a prescribed order. Rituals can be part of your daily routine without you even realizing it, such as how you make your coffee and where you sit to drink it. Or they can be intentional marks of passages for events or transitions, to invoke blessings or protection, or to express devotion or gratitude. Rituals can also create a sense of connection with the divine. Rituals are typically characterized by their symbolic significance and may involve prayers, chants, gestures, offerings, and other symbolic acts.

Conducting a spell is creating a specific form of ritual intended to bring about a particular outcome or change through magical or spiritual energy. Both

How to Get Started with Rituals and Spells

rituals and spells involve intentional actions performed for spiritual purposes; the critical difference lies in the intent and focus: Rituals are often broader in scope, serving to connect individuals with the sacred or to mark significant moments, and spells are more specific, aiming to manifest outcomes through shifting energy.

It's important to know the difference because rituals can be adjusted and molded to fit what feels right to you, but spells are more of a recipe that should be followed in order to see the full impact. Rituals are harder to track the intended outcome and will result in more of a shift in feeling, thinking, and being. Spells should be followed with the intention of tracking the outcome to know if it worked.

All spells are a type of ritual, but not all rituals are spells.

I often speak of spells as being a form of prayer, but there is also a difference between praying and spell casting. When we pray to God, the Goddess, deities, or any outside source, we ask an entity outside of us to bring us aid or comfort. We give it up to them to show us the way, to create the change, or to grant our request. Spells, on the other hand, are not about asking someone outside of you for help or to enact a change. When you do spell work, you are commanding the change through your own powerful will, choices, and intentions.

Your will is a powerful creation tool, more powerful than relying solely on an external entity. You are already creating, all the time, through your energy and thoughts. The idea with a spell is to make them intentional so that what you create aligns with what you've discovered about yourself and what you desire. Remember that when you change, your circumstances will change, and when you add a layer of spell casting along with the change, you are tapping into all the energy the North (or any direction you are working with) has to offer you.

Part Two of the book is laid out in a specific way that allows you to build on your practice. Setting up your sacred space and altars will help you with rituals and spells further in this section. For example, if you want to call on your ancestors when you are reconnecting to your body, you will work the ancestor rituals first, then when you get to the body rituals, they will be primed and ready.

At any point, you may choose to work with just one area and focus on it for a period of time. Or you may choose to go deep into each area and implement each facet of what I'm providing all at once. You are a sovereign being, and this is your path, and you should move at the pace that feels comfortable to you.

Chapter Thirteen
Definitions

Journaling

There are many instances in Part One where I asked you to use a journal or to write something down. Writing all your experiences down is important, as it allows you to track what is taking place and clears your mind of clutter. Regular journaling—used to process your thoughts, feelings, and experiences—should be a daily practice. Journaling about the outcome of rituals and spells is equally important.

I suggest a daily journal that is part of how you process your life and a secondary journal that is used to track your rituals and spells. If you want a journal that is specific to this path, you can find my *Sacred Magic: A Witch's Journal* in Resources in Part Three.

Sacred Magic

Divination: Divination is the sacred practice of uncovering hidden knowledge and receiving guidance from the spiritual realm, spirit guides, or even your own intuition. It is the art of interpreting symbols or patterns to unlock truths about yourself or a particular question you might have. Divination bypasses your mind. Whether through tarot or oracle cards, scrying, astrology, runes, or other ancient methods, divination serves as a pathway to deeper spiritual exploration and connection. It allows us to transcend the ordinary and open ourselves to the wisdom of higher powers, guiding our soul's journey with clarity and intention.

For this book of the North we will explore two types of divination: The first is working with an oracle or tarot deck. If you are new to this and do not have a deck to start with, you can find my *Sacred Magic: A Witch's Oracle Deck* that is made specifically to support this work. (See Resources in Part Three.) You can also visit a local metaphysical store or shop online and choose one that speaks to you. There are many options, and I suggest you choose one based on the colors and symbols that align for you.

In the Moon Temple Mystery School, where I teach and provide the teachings of sacred magic, witchcraft, and spiritual awakenings, I also have classes that are a deeper dive into tarot and oracle cards. (See Resources in Part Three.)

The second type of divination we will explore is using your body as the indication of yes or no to any question you want to know. We covered this when you practiced learning your body's yes and your body's no. Another way to think about this is to see your body as a pendulum. A pendulum is a tool used to ask yes or no questions. You hold a hanging item on a string, and depending on which way it sways, an answer is gained. For this book we will do that with our body and not with an outside tool.

Definitions

Offerings

You will often hear me speak of providing an offering to a spirit, ancestor, or being from the spiritual world that is nonhuman. Regardless of what spirit or energetic being you are connecting with, an offering is a foundational practice to all the rituals I'm including here. Offerings come in many forms and can be complex and thoughtful or as simple as an intentional breath.

Offerings are a sacred practice similar to how we leave flowers at the graves of people we love. It is an honoring of connection and an exchange of energy. It may seem strange when I ask you to leave a piece of fruit or a beverage on your altar that will never be physically consumed, but it works and the spirit will take the energy from the offering as a token of your gratitude. Think of an offering as a way of showing respect and gratitude, just as you might take a gift when visiting someone's home or offer refreshment when they visit yours; it's a kind and welcoming thing to do.

An offering also creates a form of reciprocity for exchanging energy with you. If you are asking spirits for knowledge, wisdom, protection, or just awareness of who is there, fostering a reciprocal exchange is important—as it is in any relationship. If you approach offerings as a demonstration of your willingness to give and receive, the connection becomes stronger faster.

You should carefully consider your offering before you proceed, as once you give it, you should treat the item as no longer yours. No matter what it is, once you've given an item as an offering, it is not to be kept, as it is no longer yours. There is a difference between putting an item on your altar to honor a loved one versus providing an offering. Once you give an offering, if it's a reusable item, you should donate it or leave it randomly in some place for someone else to receive it. Because the offering will no longer be yours, make sure the item is not something you want to keep.

Once you decide what offering to provide, you need to choose a location. For land spirits, I can usually find a place outdoors, such as by a tree or on a deck. If you cannot leave it outside, find a special place indoors.

When you provide an offering to a spirit, you should write down or speak who it is for, what it is for, and where you will leave it. Speak their name and say something like, "Spirit guide, thank you for being with me and please accept this offering as a token of my gratitude." Take a few deep breaths, picturing the spirit receiving it, then place it in the location you have chosen.

Never let any offering get moldy or stale. Once you feel the offering is complete (if you're not sure, go with one or two days), if it's a food or biodegradable item, take it outside and bury it or place it on the Earth. Speak the words, "Please accept the remnants of this sacred offering." If it's an item such as an old watch, a coin, or an item of yours, give it away or donate it once the offering is complete. If you placed the offering on a plate or in a glass (such as a glass of whiskey for the land spirits), pour the contents out, then wash the plate or glass.

Here are some other ideas when considering offerings.

- Research the history of who has lived on your lands and what they farmed or what they had at that time. It's often tobacco or grain alcohol. These make great offerings.
- If you are connecting with a specific spirit (such as an ancestor), think of the time they were alive and what was a common food or beverage and the location they came from.
- Focus on fresh fruits that are in season so they have significance to the time of year.
- Consider what you have that represents the various elements. For example, for Earth you may have a special crystal or item made of wood you would like to offer.
- If nothing feels just right or you aren't sure, your voice is one of the most powerful offerings you can give, especially when you use heartfelt words, poems, or songs. Singing to a spirit is a gift that lasts many lifetimes.

Definitions

Remember that once you provide an offering, it's no longer yours and you should treat it as such. If you desire to keep an item, use the item as a token of remembrance or honoring on an altar but not as an offering.

Candles and incense

Let's take a quick look at working with fire magic and candles. I will reference their use in a few of the rituals ahead, although a deeper dive into working with fire will occur in the third book of the series on the South. As we explore these rituals and begin working on embodiment, keep fire safety top of mind. It's easy to move into altered states and forget you have a candle burning. Never leave a candle burning without being fully present. Ensure the candle is on a heat-safe plate in case it drips and exercise the same caution when working with charcoal or incense or when burning plants. Use caution and physically stay with anything that is lit or burning.

The easiest way to learn how to make your own incense is to use incense charcoal discs, which can be found online. After lighting, you should leave the charcoal for a few moments until it turns gray and has a layer of ash over it, then slowly add the incense (blend of plants and herbs) you are using. The first time you do this you will notice the charcoal burns them up very quickly, as you are placing the incense directly on a hot coal. Once you have used a charcoal and some ash has gathered in your heat-safe bowl, you can scoop a little of the ash on top of the charcoal before adding your incense. That slows how fast it will burn and will allow your plants and herbs to burn more slowly.

Make sure you have a heat-safe burn bowl or find one made for incense. Leave the ash in the bowl each time you use it until it gets full. Once it's full and completely cooled, take it outdoors and offer it to the Earth. You can sprinkle or bury it and say, "Please receive this sacred offering."

Sourcing Supplies

One of the most common questions I get is where to buy the supplies. My answer is always to start by shopping local if you need anything new. Find a local metaphysical store, magic shop, or occult store. Most shops will help you find the supplies you are looking for such as dried plants, heat-safe bowls, candles, or even a preblended incense. Remember to ask where the supplies come from and do your best to find ethically sourced supplies.

Another option to source items is Etsy. Many handicrafters on Etsy make incense by hand from their own gardens. There are also many types of journals and custom products you might like on the site.

You should take the same approach to sourcing local for crystals, candles, premade teas, or seeds. Find a local store first before shopping online. Crystals especially are good to hold and touch before you buy them. I will not provide a list of what crystals to use when; instead I encourage you to find a place to go to in-person and test them with your own body. Choose what gives you a little tingle when you hold it or find ones of a color that draws your eye. There is no wrong way to use crystals.

Much of what you will need for the rituals and spells in this book can be found in nature around you. Even if you live in a city, there is likely a park close by or a garden center where you can walk through, touch, and find items that will suit your needs. A rock you find when on a hike is just as powerful as any crystal you might buy.

When it comes to sacred spaces and altars, you likely already have what you need to create these. The goal isn't to go buy more things but instead to find the items you have that carry the most meaning for you. What has the most meaning for you will create a more powerful altar, as these items already contain the energy of you and your emotions. When you buy something new, it has someone else's energy or is void of any connection. Start with what you have before looking for items to buy for an altar or sacred space.

Now let's slowly and purposefully move into rituals and spells.

Chapter Fourteen
Digital Detoxing

WE START HERE with disconnecting from the external noise and influence of the world to step into spaces that allow us to see, feel, and experience sacred magic. You won't find magic by scrolling social media or responding to the continual noises and vibrations from your phone. You certainly will not be able to connect to nature if you are continually interrupted with text message notifications, and you will definitely not be able to connect with spirits if you are constantly looking at other people's posts on Facebook, Instagram, or TikTok.

You can do the work of detoxing from your addiction to your devices—I promise you can. You may find it hard at first then be super disappointed when you realize you are actually addicted to your phone. The first step is to try, slowly and daily, noticing how uncomfortable you are when you begin. This is normal. I promise you that feeling like you are literally detoxing from a drug is normal. Keep trying and keep extending the time away from your phone and social media. The process of digitally detoxing is one of the greatest acts of magic you will ever perform!

We live in a time when we've replaced our intuition with an app's information. We have allowed ourselves to become so addicted to the alerts of our phone that when we start to disconnect, we actually feel like we are detoxing. Trust me, I know this to be true for myself and the thousands of students to whom I have taught this fundamental ritual. It's not just me preaching about the addiction of our devices; you can read any scientific report coming out about addiction, and you'll see cell phones, social media, and digital sources are at the top of the list.

Digital Detox Ritual

This ritual will help you disconnect from the noise of digital distraction. You can do this, I promise. The ritual starts with a few minutes a day, leads to a few hours a week, and builds to a full day a month. Here's an overview.

1. Start with turning off all devices and listening to your own thoughts and body ten minutes a day. You can sit in stillness or sit in nature during this time. If you are not used to sitting in stillness, you may want to walk or move your body. Don't be surprised when you start doing this that your mind immediately starts going through its to-do list or the stresses of the day. This is normal, and if you have never meditated before, I recommend finding a guided meditation online to help you take this break. There are many free sources of meditations on places like YouTube. Schedule this time in your calendar and mark

it as digital-free; good times for this are when you first wake up, over your lunch break, or in the evening before bed. Do this for thirty days without needing to journal or perform any rituals afterward. Spend just ten minutes a day of nothing but you and you.

2. In the second month, increase the time without any devices scrolling social media, shopping online, or checking your phone to thirty minutes a day. As in the first step, no notifications are allowed, no phone, no music, no audiobook—just the quiet between you and you. Do not feel that you must journal afterward; don't add this in yet. Let your mind and body connect and your senses continue to awaken. Do this for thirty days. The more time you sit with yourself, the deeper your processing will be, and the more your senses will come alive. You can sit in stillness or in nature during this time.

3. Continue with thirty minutes a day in the third month and begin to find a two-hour slot in your weekly schedule. You may want to move and walk during this time or dance or sing. Still no devices or external input—just you and you. During this step, you are finding two hours a week without any devices or noise (other than that of your family or nature). You might clean, do other rituals in this book, journal, walk, or dance. The goal is no digital devices. Afterward, notice if it was hard. How often did you want to reach for your phone? What did you hear or see? What did your mind process? How did your body feel? Journal if you'd like or simply pay attention, be present, and note everything. Use this time to begin working on the practices and rituals that connect you to nature and your body.

4. The next level of detoxing from external noise in order to hear more of your own wisdom is where the real magic begins to show itself and requires you to do a full day without digital devices. Plan a day with fun activities, alone or with loved ones (as long as they agree to no devices). Once a month, allow yourself a day to play and experience

the world around you with no digital influences. This is also a good day to do magic rituals and spells such as on a full moon or a new moon. It can also be a regular Sunday when you choose to recharge your own energy resources and feel deeply into the world around you. This is possible, and the world will not fall apart without your being online for a day. As you did with the two-hour slots, notice how often you wanted to reach for your phone. Did you start to get itchy to get back online? Addiction to our devices is real and when you spend your first full day without them, you'll learn this for yourself.

Chapter Fifteen
Sacred Spaces and Altars

The spaces we live and work in are alive with energy. Our homes, offices, and even vehicles contain and hold power. The energy of all physical spaces can either connect you to your intentions or work against what you want to feel. It's critical to put in the time and attention to create sacred spaces with thought and care. The size, location, or type of material doesn't matter—it's all energy. Wood, shingles, bricks, and metal are all vibrational energy fields.

Start with focusing on your entire home; make your space sacred with the rituals included, then move to the creation of altars. Whether you start with one main altar or several altars is entirely up to you. We'll start with cleaning—removing old clutter and items we no longer need and making our space a sacred reflection of what we truly feel and desire. Once that is complete, we will move to creating altars that will hold the intentions of the connection we want for ourselves, our loved ones, plants, elements, and spirits.

Sacred Cleaning Ritual

1. Set enough time aside to do your cleaning as a devotional practice. Turn on your favorite music or podcast and gather your supplies. This is a great time to be in one of the phases of digital detoxing, except you may have music playing.
2. Go slowly as you clean. Dance and move your body. Pick up the items in areas you are dusting and express gratitude for them.
3. When washing windows or counters, spray your cleaner in the shape of a heart and say thank you.
4. When you are cleaning, hold the feeling of gratitude and love to improve your connection to your space.
5. If spaces feel void of energy or carry heavy energy, commence with a smoke cleansing ritual when cleaning is done (the steps can be found in the Plant Allies section).
6. Focus on cleaning as an act of connecting with your space. It's a wonderful practice to bring the family or roommates along for this ritual and make it a dance party for everyone.

Clearing Ritual One Box at a Time

As described in the Sacred Spaces of the North chapter, do this ritual at least twice a year. Go into all the corners, closets, and places in your home (garage too) and remove old items that are holding negative energy, filling one box at a time. If you don't use an item or don't love it—don't keep it. You likely have built up stuff in all corners of your house, and this can create heavy, dense energy in your home. The clutter or unwanted items definitely don't help you find and experience sacred magic. This usually happens over time without us realizing it, but once you do realize it and there's stuff in every corner, it can feel like a daunting task to get started. One box at a time is a way to make it easier without the pressure to do it all at once and it helps to do it with intention.

1. Plan for this to take weeks or months so it isn't overwhelming on the first day. Gather a bunch of boxes and set them aside.
2. Take one box out; you may even wish to write inside the box with a marker, "Thank you for your time with me, but it's time for you to go." I also suggest you carry a trash bag for the items that are garbage. The box can be for items to donate or give away.
3. Take the box and the bag and pick one place to start. You may wish to start in one room, one closet, or one area of the kitchen; it doesn't really matter. If you don't know where to start, find the cardinal North of each room and start there.
4. Turn music on and make it joyful.
5. Go through the selected section of your home and pick up every item and ask yourself if it has meaning or if it's just collecting dust. Then box it, trash it, or clean it and put it back. If you're working in a closet, organize it as you go.
6. When the box is full, decide where it's going and finish the box by delivering it. Throw the garbage away.
7. Do not be surprised if it feels so good that you end up filling another box at the same time.
8. Keep practicing this ritual until you have done it through each part of your home.

Creating Altars

Altars themselves are rituals. Altars are rituals in which we focus on matching a particular area of our home or any space with the energy of how we want to feel in that space. The different types of altars covered here are merely recommendations to start; you can change them, add to them, or do them entirely differently. Altars are an extension of you, so let them be as unique as you are.

At this point in your stay in the magical wonders of the North, you are likely feeling the deep call to connect to nature. Many people see nature as outside their home, but you can bring nature inside too. By connecting to the element of Earth as described in this book, you have done the great work of bringing the mysteries to life.

If you've learned anything so far, I hope it includes the awareness that the Earth is an energy that is alive and can be utilized in every aspect of your life. You can bring this alive energy inside with indoor plants of any kind. Almost everyone can have at least one plant (I have hundreds) indoors. Not only will it improve circulation and bring positive energy into your home, but it will also put you in touch with our connection to Earth. The plants need water, just like you. The plants need sun, just like you. The plants need care, just like you. And plants will cycle through stages of losing their leaves, just as we cycle through the changes we experience and shed old parts of ourselves for new growth. As a reminder, add Earth elements to each altar and update and change them often with fresh Earth items.

Each book in this series will have ideas for altars, and you may find that you keep separate altars for each direction, creating magical points of energy in each cardinal direction, or you combine them all.

Your altars are an extension of you and can be anything you want them to be. They should be fluid and evolve as you evolve. As you work closer with your space and make it as sacred as you desire, you can tune into each one and feel when it's stale and needs a change. Of course, like all clearings of your home, they should be cleaned regularly and recharged often.

My personal practice is to visit all my altars one by one during each full moon. I sit with them, clean them, add to them, remove what doesn't feel right, and infuse them with my own energy and love.

Your Personal Altar

Finding indoor and outdoor space for devotion to nature is life changing. These altars may or may not be placed in the cardinal direction of the North—it doesn't matter for this practice. This stop on the spiral path of sacred magic, which starts in the North, will take you deep into the Earth and deep into your body. Let's call this your personal altar.

1. To start an altar for yourself, find a shelf, box, table, counter, or any space and obtain a picture of yourself or several pictures. Let the picture be a reflection of what you've learned about yourself in this book.
2. Surround the picture with items representing the North (you can add other directional items as you continue your journey through the next books). You do not need to buy anything for your personal altar; use items you already have that represent you. No matter the weather outside, you can bring a piece of your land to your altar. If it's snowing, scoop up some clean snow and add it to a glass on your altar. If it's sunny and the trees are in bloom, look for something they have dropped on the ground for you. Rocks, sticks, plants—anything from your land—along with the picture of you are great starting places.
3. Visit your personal altar during the Digital Detox Ritual, while doing any of the other rituals in this book, and as a place to pray or meditate. The goal is for this to be a place to express yourself and go deeply inward.
4. If you want to create a balanced altar with all the elements on your personal altar, by all means do so. Below I briefly list some possible items for each direction. You can lay out your personal altar like this:

Put items (like pictures) that represent yourself in the middle and place items from the North that represent the Earth at the top of this space. To the right (East) of your items add a representation of the element of air. Below the items of yourself (South) add things that represent fire. To the left of your personal items (West), add elements of water.

Cardinal Direction Altars

Take a moment to explore the cardinal directions in any space where you spend significant time, be it your home or office. Start with one room and consider how it fits in the whole picture. Your home as a whole has a section that is to the North; each individual room, hallway, or space also has a section to the North.

This exploration can open up new dimensions in the practice of sacred magic. You may find your house to the North is all windows, walls, or hallways, or any such combination. In your bedroom, for example, look at what sits to the North of that one room. Does it support your connection to your body and the Earth? Room by room, check the cardinal direction of North in that space and ask yourself if it reflects your connection to the North. Some helpful questions are: Does the space to the North reflect you and the aspects of your path of seeking real magic at that moment? Is there balance in the space? How does the space feel in your body?

I often recommend adding an item from the Earth, such as a bowl of salt, to the northern parts of each room to help the energy in that room be balanced and grounded. You can use stones, wood, or anything from nature that feels grounding to you. Here are some ideas for the North sections of rooms: For your living room, add something special from nature such as a plant. For your bedroom, place a small stone or a pinecone you found on a walk. For your kitchen, bring in something made of wood. And so on.

Each book in this series will go deeper into the other elements but here are a few extra examples if you want to create a balance of the elements on your altars now.

Cardinal North is everything I've just described above.

Cardinal East represents the element of air. When you are going through your home, you can add feathers, words you've written, or small items like bells or wind chimes. You can even use the East in any room to store or hold your incense burn bowl.

Cardinal South represents the element of fire. Identify places opposite of North in your home to add a candle, something red, or anything that represents your passions or longings.

Cardinal West represents the element of water. The easiest way to bring this element into any room is a small glass (or chalice) of water. Find a place where pets or children will not get to it, such as the tops of shelves or above your stove or fridge. Make sure you freshen it regularly. Other items like shells, river rocks, or anything blue will bring in the element of water.

Outdoor Altar

Find a place in nature to call your own for the next several weeks. If you have property and weather allows, designate a place with a circle of stones or twigs and make this your Earth altar. Bring special items or offerings to the land such as tobacco, tea, plants, or personal items (your voice, a strand of hair). Connect, feel, or do any of the rituals in this book in your outdoor space. If you do not have outdoor space to make a permanent altar, find a park bench, a patch of grass, a fresh field of snow, or any place that is natural and sit with it. Bring an offering that can be left behind or just dedicate a few breath cycles to the space.

Ancestor Altar

Ancestors are closely present at all times and can be accessed easily if you choose for them to be. It's not a complicated ritual or ceremony that brings these loving beings into our awareness. If you want to connect to your ancestors for the first time, an altar is the perfect place. An ancestor altar can be as simple or detailed as you want.

Keep in mind that any ancestors who may not have made the best choices in their lifetime as humans have left that behind when they entered the spiritual realm. They may remain a bit sassy or can be funny, but if they left you with trauma of any kind, know that they will wish peace upon you from where they are now. And if you still don't want to connect with them during your ancestral workings, just tell them so. You get to choose and your boundaries in the spiritual realm are real and trump anything they may want, even if what they want is to make peace.

Here's how to create your ancestor altar:

1. Find a shelf or small space to place items that represent your ancestors.
2. Start with researching everything you can find out about your lineage. Some of us may have a lineage that is untraceable and that is 100 percent OK. Find what you can and know that the rest will come through in your practice.
3. If you know with whom you want to connect, write down their name and see if you can locate pictures or items connected to that person. Add them to your altar.
4. Consider the foods your ancestors would have eaten and make those recipes, speaking to them while cooking. Add a small amount of what

you make or items related to what they would have eaten on your ancestor altar (as an offering). Leave it for a short period of time so the food does not become stale. Throw it away when complete, or better, bury it or, if it's something that won't rot, leave it outside for food offerings.
5. Write the ancestor a letter with your questions and gratitude for sharing their bloodline with you. Place it on the altar.
6. Ask them to help resolve patterns that no longer serve your family. Ask them for blessings, insight, or anything from your bloodline that would be supportive to know in your life.
7. Journal as a freewriting practice. Freewriting means setting your mind aside and letting your pen flow. Whatever comes out (sometimes even a grocery list might come out) keep going. When you've emptied your mind of the surface-level buildup of thoughts (or seemingly pressing lists), your ancestors can speak to you through your writing. Ask a question, either out loud or written down, and then just write. No wrong answers here, only practice.

Most important, remember that they want to see the blood of their blood be successful and live a life of fulfillment. They are invested in your having it easier than they did. For you, they want more joy and more success, and for you not to repeat the patterns your lineage may have carried. They are 100 percent in support of you!

Chapter Sixteen
The Spirits

This section includes rituals and methods to connect with spirits, including the spirit of the North itself, the spirit of the lands, and the spirit of your ancestors. And there are other spirits you may want to connect to, such as a friend or family member who passed away, a spirit that dwells in your home for unknown reasons, or even your spirit guides (which I will cover in the East of this series).

Certain spirits correspond to each direction of sacred magic and its element. Here in the North we are working with land spirits and ancestors. Spirits to the East include angels and archangels, to the South are goddesses, and to the West we find water spirits and spirit guides. Although the rituals will be slightly different for each element, if one of these calls to you at this stage, you may use these rituals as a template for any spirit you want to connect to.

Ritual to Connect to the Spirit of the North

To connect to the energy of the North is to connect to the Earth. There are many ways to do it, and you have already begun this process if you've read this far in the book. The North calls to you as much as you call to it.

This isn't complicated magic; this is connecting to yourself and asking what you need.

1. Start by setting an intention of sitting with the North for a period of time. I usually recommend at least seven days, and twenty-one is better. Find a time frame between the two that you can commit to for at least thirty minutes per day. This is the perfect time to also be in the Digital Detox Ritual.
2. Set the intention and mark your calendar, clear your schedule, and commit.
3. Turn off all devices and be fully present to the North.
4. Connect to the elemental spirit of the North by speaking something like, "Hello, North spirit, I am here with you in full surrender and am open to receive your wisdom."
5. Have a journal and pen or pencil handy, ask any of the following questions, and let the answers flow out of you. If no answers come while writing, write the question sentence over and over until something comes.

Questions:

Where do I feel ease in my body?

Where do I feel tension? Why?

Where do I need more rest?

What feels heavy in my life right now? Why?

How can I honor my body and its connection to the Earth?

Again, if no answer comes, write whatever comes after saying, "I am with you in full surrender to the North."

The Spirits

6. In between the daily sessions, pay attention to how the Earth speaks to you. It will come by feelings in your body, such as your eyes water a lot (a sign you need to rest your mind because you cannot see clearly) your shoulders ache (a sign you are sitting too long in one spot), or your hips feel tight when you bend over (you need to move or walk, and loosen up). Look for the signals from your body the element of the North will show you.
7. Once the days you committed to are complete, review what you have written and take a new page and write a story about your time in the North. Start it with "My time in the North was ..." and summarize everything.

Ritual to Connect with the Spirits of the Lands

This is a ritual I teach to many people, and I recommend everyone work with the spirits of the lands where they live. There is no downside to thanking land spirits; you cannot do too much of it. We are living on the lands of others, and whether we own property, rent a room, or live nomadically, learning to connect with your current location, creates an entirely new flow and peaceful alignment in your life. It impacts everything you touch and everything you do because it impacts *you*.

1. Start by researching the location in which you live (or are visiting if you have travel plans). Write down everything you can find: tribal history, foods that may have been farmed, any historical events that occurred there. Everything you find will give you insight into that special place on the planet.
2. Write a statement of intent to connect to the spirits of the lands. Ask them to connect with you and explain why. An example: "Dear spirits

Sacred Magic

of the lands that I call home, thank you for welcoming me to the space where you roam. I would like to connect with you to learn how to be a good steward of this slice of the Earth. I would like my home to feel safe, loving, and protected. Please help me with this."

3. If you are asking for something specific, such as a happy home, harmony with the lands, wisdom, insight, or whatever it is, write it out and include what you are offering in return.
4. Set up an altar or special place; this can be inside or outside your home.
5. Keep a candle on your altar (while indoors) and light it when you are communicating.
6. Make offerings over and over again. This is important and they will bless you in return.
7. Speak to the spirits of the lands whenever you pass from your home to the outside world, even if it's just a simple acknowledgment in your mind or spoken aloud: "Thank you, land spirits."
8. As with all spirit rituals, they aren't necessarily going to communicate with you only when you are in the ritual itself, especially if you are visiting your altar or speaking to them only once a week or a month. The spirits you are connecting to will communicate with you outside of the ritual during your day-to-day life.

Walking Ritual to Connect with the Spirits of the Lands

Here's another option for connecting to the spirits of the lands.

1. Walk the perimeter of your property or outside of your building if you reside in an apartment. Ask to connect with the spirits of the lands. If possible, leave small token items in each direction to say thank you for allowing you to dwell where they once did.

The Spirits

2. Know the cardinal directions when walking the perimeter so when you are in each direction, you can provide an offering from that element. For example, in the North, a piece of hair, a soft song or chant, a sprig of rosemary, or any Earth connection. In the East, drop a small feather or penny or offer a soft song or chant. To the South, tobacco, a dash of cinnamon, or even a small piece of cookie. To the West, any type of liquid, such as gin or rum, or share your coffee/tea.
3. Walk the perimeter with these items in your hands, in your pockets, or on a tray and leave the items as you reach each cardinal direction.

Ritual to Connect with Your Ancestors

Connecting to your ancestors is powerful work and can be approached in a few simple ways. First complete the altar and steps for an Ancestor Altar above. Take your time on the research and setting up a space to honor them (both the known and unknown bloodlines on both sides of your families).

When you want to connect to your ancestors, think of it as a time to sit around a fire and share stories and wisdom.

1. Near your ancestor altar (you do not need to be directly in front of it but close enough to light a candle and be able to monitor it for safety), find a comfortable place to sit and make sure you are in a quiet space and will not be disturbed for thirty minutes.
2. Close your eyes and spend five minutes breathing deeply so your body relaxes and your heart slows down.
3. When you feel your body is relaxed, in your mind's eye picture yourself sitting by a fire with your mother to your left and your father to your right. Beyond both of them sit their parents. You can visualize as far back in your lineage as you want, but I recommend you begin with just one parent and their parents at a time. Keeping your eyes closed,

say hello and introduce yourself. See if any images or thoughts come into your mind. Hold this visual for as long as you can, then open your journal and write down what occurred.

This is a specific visualization practice to see your lineage one at a time. Don't rush the process and come back often. If you hit a blank space when visualizing, keep trying. It will come.

Chapter Seventeen
Elemental Rituals

To start working with the element of the North, the Earth, very simply you must begin by taking yourself outdoors. Taking yourself outdoors and being in the element of Earth seems easy, yet how many times in the course of a week do you go outside only to get to your car or go someplace else and barely notice that nature is alive all around you? Even when the weather is stormy or cold, you can connect to the Earth when you go outdoors and take a gigantic breath of air into your lungs, look up at the sky above you, look around you at the state of nature in the moment, and be in full presence. This is a must if you want to truly understand the element of the North.

Other ways to connect to the Earth element are to bring items inside your home, sit outdoors, have picnics, build altars, use plants as medicine, and ground into the soil. The list is endless. I share examples of rituals that are specific to the element of Earth, but I want you to keep in mind that being outside on its own is a ritual if you approach it with the intention of connecting to the element of Earth. We'll also explore spells such as seeds of intention, stone magic, and the roses of death. These are all starting points, and they can be used for anything you need to process in your life or any material item you wish to call into your life. Manifesting, clearing energy, creating joy, and finding peace and abundance—all of it can be sourced in nature.

Elemental Healing Ritual

I shared this ritual I did when I was writing my memoir and shifted the energy from the time weaving, which left me decimated with pain from calling forth the memories. Although I used this in an emergency, it can also be something you plan. Whatever is happening in the moment, first know that you want to give yourself space and time to feel it fully before you process it physically or perform any rituals with the elements. Make sure you have time and privacy to let it all out.

1. Prepare whatever elements you have access to. For the North, either plan to take it outside or bring Earth to you—plants, soil, flowers, branches, or anything you can forage for. For the East (air), we'll use our breath, but you can also burn incense or plant allies. For the South, light candles for fire or make a fire if possible. For the West, a bath or shower will work—or water in nature (especially rain or snow).
2. If it's urgent, make a rough plan in your mind. If you have more time to plan and create the ritual, then do so. Gather your items and turn off all devices, except turn on music that represents how you feel.

3. Go into the feelings—whatever they may be. Let your body move and express how the feelings feel. Stomp, yell, shake, swear, jump up and down, roll on the floor, twerk, or make any movement of your body the emotions inspire. The point is to move with your emotions. I find music helps—if you're angry, find angry music; if you're sad, use sad music. If you're over-the-top excited and cannot contain your joy, turn on your favorite dance music. Keep feeling, emoting, and moving until you feel your body become tired and empty of emotion.
4. Then begin with the Earth. Go to the Earth and sit with it or bring part of it against your skin. Just sink into the Earth and let it sink into you.
5. Then move to the element of air and start deep breathing, relaxing your body. Burn incense or herbs and smell them deeply. Slow the music if you have any playing and slow your breathing. If there are words you want to speak to yourself, speak them now, softly. Stay in nature as long as needed until you feel lighter.
6. Then move to fire—watch the flame, any flame, and picture any remaining emotion burning away.
7. Finish with water by showering or taking a bath. Picture all the sweat, tears, pain, and emotion finally washing down the drain.
8. When you've finished the ritual, take time with yourself to nourish your body. You may be hungry, thirsty, or super tired. Take a nap and eat foods that will feed your body with nutrients and comfort.

This ritual can be used for any big change you experience in your life. I teach this to many of my clients as a way to handle stress that cannot be shaken off or when they are so excited about something they cannot seem to focus. It's not only deep pain that the elements can heal; they also can bring balance and perspective to any situation. Once you try this ritual, it likely will become a part of how you handle any big swing of emotion in your life.

Learning How to Ground

If you've ever gone for a walk when you felt stressed or anxious, you know how powerful just being outdoors is. That itself is a grounding ritual. Grounding is a fundamental concept in this book. It is what the North represents, and it is the medicine we have available to us just by going outside. It's a process of connecting your body's energy with the Earth's energy.

Learning how to do grounding rituals is the fastest way to restore balance create stability, and allow a sense of presence. All grounding practices should have the intention of alignment and moving energy that needs to go, as both matter.

Grounding will help you center and stabilize your energy. Grounding will also help you come back to the present moment and be connected to the cycles in all things. It reminds us that, whether we like it or not, this too shall pass.

The other reason why grounding is critical is because when we do big ritual work or spell work, we're doing it from a place of heightened energy. We raise the energy then perform our work. If we do not ground our energy afterward, it can be a bumpy road back into our normal day-to-day tasks.

Here are three rituals to use for grounding yourself.

Rooting Meditation

1. Find a quiet and comfortable space where you won't be disturbed. Sit or lie down in a relaxed position and close your eyes.
2. Take several deep breaths, inhaling through your nose and exhaling through your mouth, allowing your body to relax with each breath.
3. Visualize roots extending from the soles of your feet deep into the Earth, anchoring you firmly.
4. Feel the stability and support of the Earth's energy as it flows up through your roots and into your body.
5. Spend several minutes in this grounded state, absorbing the Earth's nurturing energy and releasing any tension or stress.

Walking Barefoot Ritual

1. Find a safe outdoor location where you can walk barefoot, such as a park or garden.
2. Stand barefoot on the Earth and take a few deep breaths to center yourself.
3. As you walk, focus on the sensation of the Earth beneath your feet, paying attention to the texture, temperature, and energy exchange.
4. With each step, imagine yourself drawing in the Earth's energy through the soles of your feet, filling your body with grounding and revitalizing energy.
5. Continue walking for as long as it feels comfortable, allowing yourself to fully connect with the Earth and absorb its healing vibrations.

Crystal Grid Grounding Ritual

1. Gather grounding crystals, such as black tourmaline, hematite, or smoky quartz. If you don't have these, find any rocks that feel good when you hold them. You can forage for grounding stones or purchase them.
2. Find a quiet space where you can set up your crystal grid.
3. Place a large grounding stone, such as a black tourmaline (or any black stone), at the center of your grid.
4. Surround the central stone with smaller grounding crystals, arranging them in a circle or other geometric pattern.
5. Sit or stand near your crystal grid and take several deep breaths to center yourself.
6. Focus your attention on the energy of the crystals, feeling their grounding and protective properties enveloping you.
7. Visualize roots extending from your body into the Earth, connecting you with the grounding energy of the crystals and the Earth itself.

8. Spend as much time as you like in the presence of your crystal grid, allowing yourself to absorb its grounding energy and find a sense of stability and balance.

Tree Magic

As we explore the North deeper and deeper, we begin to see the connection between the Earth and our body. As we connect to our body and connect to the Earth, a whole new world opens between us and all living things. Yet there is an area that is often missed when spending time with Earth rituals and spells, and that is the power of working with trees.

For this ritual, I recommend you find one spot outdoors and commit to thirty days of sitting in the same place with the same tree. As with the Outdoor Altar, this is if space and weather permit. Any tree will do. I have done this many times over the years, and when you visit the same tree every day, the tree begins to open up and commune with you in a way you never knew was possible. It will change how you interact with nature. It will change how nature interacts with you.

1. Find a tree that you can sit with comfortably.
2. Take a journal and pencil.
3. Turn off your phone and any electronic devices.
4. You can either use freewriting or ask the tree questions and write out what comes to you. It's all connected and it's all sacred.
5. Take this time to give the tree your pain, worry, or stress. Bang your fists on the ground, lie down, cry, or do whatever feels right. When you take a big emotion stored in your body and give it to the tree, it says thank you. It can hold that emotion for you.

Elemental Rituals

Soil Ritual

Yes, you'll get dirty, and that's the point. This is powerful work to do when you need healing both physically and mentally.

1. Find a patch of soil near you, and wearing a limited amount of clothes, lie down directly on the soil.
2. Picture it absorbing what ails you.
3. Hold it in your mind's eye and stay as long as you can.
4. Clean yourself up after, and as you wash away the dirt, hold the vision that all the soil being removed is removing what hurts you.
5. Journal any reflections after the ritual.

*Note: You can do this ritual in the snow, in the rain, or during any elemental situations you find yourself in when you need healing.

Earth Charm Magic

Carrying a magic spell with you feels amazing, as it is secretive and personal; it's just for you. Carrying an Earth charm is powerful and simple.

1. Create a small satchel made of anything (an old sock, a piece of a scarf) and speak your intentions of healing into the satchel while creating it.
2. Fill the satchel with fresh dirt. You may also add any plants or a small stone to the satchel.
3. Write about your intentions, especially those that are aligned with being in the North, and add them to the satchel. Then stitch it closed with a needle and thread.
4. Carry the satchel with you for at least seven days.

Sacred Magic

5. When done, take the satchel apart, give all the contents back to the Earth by simply putting them back on the ground or burying them, and dispose of the satchel.
6. Reflect on and journal about what you noticed while carrying the Earth charm.

Seeds of Intention Spell

We often do this in mystery school in the spring to create magic with seeds; there are two things to know before you do this spell. First, we plant the seeds away from us so we will not monitor them and use their growth (or lack thereof) to determine whether our intentions are cast. They are. Second, you can do this at any time of year, and either hold the seeds until planting season or bury them off-season, knowing that when the Earth wakes up, they will too.

1. Be clear about your intentions and write them out.
Have a packet of any seed nearby.
2. When your intentions are clear, hold either one or several seeds in your palm and read your intentions thirteen times while feeling the seeds in your hand.
3. Breathe into the seeds and set them aside.
4. Do this for each of your intentions.
5. Plant them away from where you will be able to watch and monitor their growth.

Stone Magic

There are dozens of books out there about crystals and what they mean; if you want a deeper dive into crystals, research as much as you want. I prefer to work with crystals intuitively. They speak to me, and I can feel their healing and physical properties just by holding and focusing on the stones. Work with crystals in ways that suit you.

Here I focus on regular old stones of nature. We come across them all the time, and they are just as powerful as any item on Earth. Many have been weathered for thousands of years and hold big energy for you to utilize in your practice.

Let's start with preparing your own stones to use for divination (meaning a tool to help you find guidance when you have questions).

1. Find two stones of a similar type. Try not to use ones that look like they have been made from broken concrete or created for gardens. These would work, but the wilder ones covered in dirt or found in remote places work best.
2. Bring them home and clean them gently. Offer words of gratitude while cleaning them.
3. Let them dry in the sun.
4. Once dry, hold one at a time and ask yourself questions you know the answer to is yes (such as your name, day of the week, things you know to be true). Then say, "This is the yes stone." Add a Y on the stone.
5. Repeat with the second stone and charge it as no with an N on it.
6. Leave these stones on any altar. When you have a yes-or-no question, with your eyes closed, shuffle them around in your hand, then choose one. This will be your answer.

Roses of Death Spell

In sacred magic, we are studying change and transformation, one direction at a time. While we are studying, we are continually exploring new ways of connecting to ourselves and our gifts. To clear space for this, there are old parts of us that need to go. A beautiful way of honoring what we are letting go of is a tender spell to let those parts of us die so new levels of magic can be reborn. I teach many spiritual death spells because every new level we awaken to requires us to let go of the last level. Every new level is a cycle of death and rebirth. This simple and powerful spell allows you to recognize that all parts of the journey matter, even the ones we are moving past.

1. Buy or find one rose per week for thirty days. Each rose is a week's worth of petals. If you cannot find a rose, use any flower that has petals you can remove one at a time.
2. Each day while doing this ritual spell, take off one at a time and write in marker anything on it that you want to let go of, such as an old habit, an old belief about yourself, disconnection from your body, a poor eating habit, or anything you want to release. Write it on a petal. Add a small bowl to your personal altar and add the petals to the bowl until the thirty days have passed.
3. At the end of the thirty days, take the bowl of petals and either bury them if you have your own property to do so or find an empty field to release them by gently sprinkling them onto the Earth.
4. Reflect on and journal about what you noticed while practicing this spell.

Chapter Eighteen
Plant Allies

PLANTS, THE ONES THAT GROW WILD and the ones we cultivate, are conduits to energetic connections. When you learn to view plants as a source of deeper connection to all living things, magical ways in which you choose to walk among them will open up, and I want you to learn about their impact for yourself. Plants aid any emotion you wish to release or call in, and they connect you to a powerful energy source. Natural items from Earth should be added to all your altar spaces, so I will not include a specific altar for plants. Instead—add them, alive or dried, everywhere.

I'll start with the fundamental work of plant allies by teaching you how to connect to any plant, regardless of where or how it grows. Then I'll move into plant brushing as a way to move energy in your body, using a bay leaf to cast intentions, smoke cleansing by burning plants, and making tea from plants of the North. I'll end with the easy, powerful way of connecting with a plant ally—creating a garden.

Connecting to Any Plant as an Ally

Here are the basic steps for connecting to the spiritual and physical properties of any plant.

1. Research the plant. If you have one outside your door or you come across one and it calls to you to learn more, find out what the plant is and do a deep dive online about any of its spiritual properties and whether it is edible. Find at least three sources and note down everything you discover.
2. Ask the plant for permission to harvest its bounty. Standing near it, ask aloud if you may take some of it to get to know the plant better. Listen to the first answer you get, such as if you immediately feel or hear a "yes" or "no." If it's a yes, take the item and leave something in its place, such as your voice, a few cycles of your breath, or even a drink of your water. If it's a no, find another item.
3. If you purchase a dried or live plant, look for local sources or those that harvest ethically.
4. Once you have the plant, add it to your altar for a few days to allow it to settle in with you.
5. Then embark on a fourteen- or twenty-one-day practice with the plant by placing a satchel filled with parts of it under your pillow, brewing a tea if you have verified it is safe to drink or eat, burning it in your charcoal bowl, or holding it while journeying.

The heart of using plants as allies lies in reverence for the spirit of plants—a strong presence that imbues each botanical entity with its unique energy and properties. The spirit of plants will communicate with you, offering guidance, healing, and protection. By forging a bond with these plant spirits, you can tap into their wisdom and utilize their energies while questing for a more fulfilling and magical life.

Plants epitomize the North with their roots firmly planted in the soil and their ability to draw sustenance from the Earth. I recommend working with one new plant ally at a time to get to know its properties and how it makes you feel spiritually, mentally, and physically before moving to another.

Track and journal all your experiences so these pieces of wisdom will be available to you in the future when you need them.

Here are two plants that are an anchoring part of my practice.

Patchouli: This plant connects you deeply to your body; in your mind it connects to immortality and rebirth, it awakens love in your heart, and it infuses your soul with attracting energy.

Mugwort: This herb steadies your nerves, strengthens digestion, and regulates hormones; in your mind it sharpens intuition, in your heart it awakens the part of you that desires to rewild, and for your soul it will call in the ancestors.

PLANT BRUSHING

This is one of the simplest and most powerful energy cleansing rituals you can do, and you can do it on the fly, anytime, anyplace.

1. All you need is a small branch from a tree with leaves or a flower. If you are foraging for this on the side of the road (as I've done often while driving), make sure you aren't taking the natural items from another person's property. If it is wild, ask the plant if it is OK to take a small piece. Trust the first response that comes to you, as described above.

2. Hold the branch or flower and brush the leaves or petals along all of your exposed skin—face, neck, arms, legs, and belly/chest. If you are alone, of course, I welcome you to strip down and brush your whole body. If you have a partner, lover, or friend with you, take turns brushing each other.
3. Give the item back to nature. The natural leaves and blooms will use their electric charge to neutralize anything you are feeling. This ritual is fast and effective.

Another way to bring this energy in throughout the day is to place a flower bud in your undergarments or a fresh flower in your hair. These powerful allies will work with you all day to create a more balanced energy, not to mention they feel and smell amazing.

Bay Leaf Magic

Bay leaves are a natural element of Earth, can be found in most grocery stores, and are a great tool for releasing energy, emotion, or anything toxic in your life, as well as for calling in something you desire. (This is a fire magic ritual and will be covered in the South book as well.) This is a simple ritual.

1. Breathe and focus on what you are releasing or calling in.
2. Hold the dried bay leaf in your palm and keep breathing until you feel your body relax.
3. Then begin focusing on the intention more intently.
4. Think it, let the feeling of the intention flood your body, and keep holding the bay leaf.
5. When you feel the emotion anchor in your body, take a marker and write out what your intention is on the bay leaf—use the front and back if needed.

Plant Allies

6. In a heat-safe bowl, burn the entire bay leaf. It will spark and crumble.
7. Stay with it until the bay leaf is gone and consider the magic in motion. Discard any cooled remains outdoors.

Note: Any dried bay leaf will work, and I prefer to use whole ones, but any part of a bay leaf is suitable.

Smoke-Cleansing Ritual

This is a baseline cleansing ritual with smoke that you can do in any space at any time as long as incense can be burned. You can burn these plants on their own without a charcoal disc, but they will not stay lit as long and you'll need to keep a lighter or matches nearby. A note about the sage needed for this ritual: Sage is overused and overcultivated so use it sparingly. If you cannot harvest your own sage, I suggest finding a local metaphysical store and ensuring that it's harvested sustainably. If you buy a bundle of sage, take it completely apart and use only a leaf or two at a time.

For supplies, you'll need: charcoal discs for incense, a small handful of any type of sage, a small handful of lavender (or rose), a heat-safe bowl or cauldron to hold the charcoal and plants, a lighter or matches, and a planned statement of intent. You can substitute local dried cedar from your lands or mugwort for the sage. The sage is to clear the space; the flowers are to infuse it with blessings.

1. Start with the statement of intent. What are you clearing and what are you adding back in? Express this in a statement like: "I cleanse and release all negative energy, allowing in only love and kindness" or "I remove any old, dense energies that no longer align with my growth and call forth opportunities and wisdom." Make it custom to what you know about the space and what you want to come into the space. I suggest keeping it short, as you'll repeat it many times during the cleansing.

Sacred Magic

2. Light the charcoal in your heat-safe bowl and stack the plants on one side of the bowl, with only a few touching the charcoal to start. Leave the rest on the side so you can move them onto the charcoal as you move through your space.
3. Start on the lowest floor of your space. Hold the bowl in your right hand and put your left hand over your heart with your palm facing to the right and your thumb against your chest. Think of it as a solid barrier against any negative energy entering your body.
4. Say your intention and burn the plants while slowly walking in a sunwise direction (keeping left hand in place) in each space, moving from lowest floor to highest.
5. Go through every room in this way and open every closet and drawer, repeating your intention. Remove your left hand from your heart only to shift more plant blend onto the charcoal.
6. Any reflective surface or mirror should be cleared three times, moving the bowl around the edges in a sunwise direction to ensure they are sealed up.
7. Go slowly and be thoughtful about your intention. This should take some time. You do not need to open any windows unless the smoke bothers anyone. The smoke itself will transmute any unwanted energy.
8. If you have other people who live in your home, you can have them walk behind you and repeat the intention with you or do the ritual when everyone is gone.
9. Additional layers after you have completed the smoke cleanse: Add an elemental representation in each cardinal direction, such as something from the Earth along any wall to the North, perhaps a small stone above a doorway or in a windowsill. To the East add something of air like a feather; to the South add something red or another item that represents fire (I leave a candle to use); to the West add a small chalice of water.

10. A final optional addition is to sprinkle a layer of salt on the outside of every door into your home. This will capture any negative energy as someone enters your home.

You can add additional protection to your home, such as burying items outdoors in each cardinal direction, but for most people, cleansing and sealing your home are enough. I suggest you do this at least once a month and anytime you feel the energy is heavy, dense, or stagnant.

Tea for the North

Teas are magical potions that bring all the elements into your body in a single ritual. They are ancient powerful spells that have been used at least as long as humans have recorded the history of natural healing. Teas are a gentle, loving way to get to know a plant and to bring its medicine into your body. It's important, however, that you do your own research before consuming any plant in any form. Also look up any medications you are on for possible drug interaction and note potential side effects before drinking tea.

When making your own tea, you can find organic sources online and in many metaphysical and natural grocery stores. Look closely at how and where the tea is harvested. Do not used packaged tea for this ritual as it often contains other plants or tea blends. Packaged tea is fine when you want a regular tea, but this is not a regular tea; this is magical tea set with intentions while you are in the North. Combining the elements of boiling water (fire and water), plants (Earth), and aromatic steam (air) with a spoken intention is a daily ritual to bring into your practice.

Use your nicest cup or mug and your finest teapot. I use large Mason jars so I can see the beauty of the plant transforming with the water. The colors and movement of the plants in the hot water are mesmerizing.

1. Set an intention. It can be simple like, "Improve my health and wellness" or "I am open to connecting to deeper wisdom with the help of these plants."
2. Focus on your intention while the water is boiling.
3. Add 1 tablespoon of plants to 1 cup of water off the boil (increase both as desired).
4. Let steep for at least five minutes, but longer is better. I often infuse mine overnight and use it the following day over ice or reheated as a magical potion to support my current endeavors.
5. Once steeped, strain it with a small metal strainer, paper towel, or a coffee filter. You can also use a traditional coffee press and press the plants before drinking.
6. Add notes to your journal on how the ritual is going and note any changes in your body and life. These will be notes you can come back to whenever you need that exact medicine again in the future.

Here are some tea combinations to try for the North. I suggest using the same blend for thirteen days before switching to another kind. Its power and how it will impact your body, spirit, and wisdom take time to be felt and recorded. You can also add a dash of honey or lemon if the taste isn't to your liking.

- Rose + Chamomile—for soothing your soul and connecting your heart to your body.
- Rose + Mugwort—for activating ancient wisdom and spiritual gifts.
- Vervain + Chamomile—for connecting Earth to your body for rest and rejuvenation.

Plant Allies

Planting an Indoor or Outdoor Garden

Another way to connect with both the magical elements of plants and the element of Earth is to grow your own magical garden we care for and study as a reflection of ourself. We tend to the soil then tend to our own body. We water the plant then water our own growth goals. We keep ourself in alignment with our garden. If we find we are ignoring it, we question if we are also ignoring our body and we explore why. Tending a garden, even if it is as simple as one pot with one seed, is a powerful way to connect yourself to nature.

For supplies, you'll need: seed(s), soil, a container for growing, and an intention statement.

1. Write a statement of your intention on how you wish to use your magical garden for your own growth.
2. Add the intention to the bottom of the planting container or in the soil where you will plant. Bury it as the foundation of what you are growing.
3. Add soil and seed(s).
4. Water and love on your magical garden.
5. As things grow, harvest and cut off parts you want to consume or save and dry or freeze them. For example, if you are growing mint in your magical garden, cut small pieces and add them to one of your ice cube trays to save and use when you want to add a little mint to your water. Each sip will be a deep connection to your intention.
6. Sit with your pot or garden often and spend time journaling and reflecting on how you are represented in your garden.

If it is not growing season in your area when you want to start your garden, find a plant that will grow indoors in a pot you can place where it's exposed to natural through a window. Be creative and visit a local garden center; there is always something that can be grown, regardless of where you live and what season it is. Do not overthink what plant you will choose. Go with your intuition. Whatever seed feels good and says yes to you, use that.

Chapter Nineteen
Body Rituals

CONNECTING TO OUR BODY is a slow process. Take one step and then another, and you will feel, see, and know where the next step should be. If you feel out of balance in your life, such as when you have a lot of moving parts going on and it feels busy and hectic, connect to your body and find out where it is impacting you physically and take time to address that part of your body. Most of us carry tension in our shoulders and necks when we are busy and haven't had time to rest or do grounding. Our body will carry the energy of what is happening in our mind. When we need to find a more balanced state of being as a whole, we must start by finding out where in our body we are carrying unwanted energy and move it out.

Remember that the body is connected to the Earth, and our spiritual and physical (and emotional) parts live inside us. To experience joy, passion, peace, and the sacredness of magic, we have to look at our body and understand how to awaken the areas we are disconnected from. Your body is the most divine temple of all temples. It is the sacred space to encounter and connect with the spiritual plane.

This section includes many ways to connect with your body. Start with one, then try another to find what creates the biggest shift between your mind and your body. If you find places of trauma or disconnection, do the work to clear the trauma. The Elemental Healing Ritual can be brought in anytime.

Daily Honoring Ritual

Start with your morning ritual and look at how you connect to your body after a long sleep. Stretch and take mental note of what parts of your body feel sore or tired. Breathe deeply and drink water to nourish your body after a long night of rest. Connect to your body and to your breath before you pick up your cell phone.

1. Start your morning with stretching, meditation, breathwork, or any practice that brings you into connection with your body.
2. Set an intention of how you want to feel in your body that day and hold the feeling while you are in morning stillness.
3. Nourish your body with a morning quench of a large glass of water after holding it to your heart and asking the water to nourish your cells.
4. As you begin to get ready for the day, speak to yourself in the mirror—or go a step further and add a love note to yourself on the mirror or attach it to the clothes in your closet. These reminders are powerful and will carry you a long way on busy days.
5. Use any ritual in this section and connect deeper.
6. At the end of your day, reconnect with your body again and ask

yourself, "Where do I feel ease and where do I feel tension?" Then honor and love on that part of your body so it can heal and reset while you sleep. This is also a great time to add in a grounding ritual as noted in the Elemental Rituals section.

Opposite-Hand Ritual

Finding a space and time in your life to reconnect to your body is important. If you are new at this, start at the beginning and work your way through these rituals. If you feel you are very strongly connected, skip to the advanced ones.

Take this ritual slowly. Many of us carry significant trauma in our body that has not yet been transmuted. If you feel anything come up for you that feels uncomfortable, take the steps to work the trauma either in therapy or with a trauma-informed coach.

1. During each shower or bath, use your favorite body wash (or make your own salt scrub) and use your opposite hand to wash the opposite side of your body. As you are washing each part of your body, thank it. Use your right hand when washing the left shoulder, saying, "Left shoulder that is a part of my flesh and bones that carry my spirit, thank you," and so on.
2. When you wash the parts that feel less than perfect, say something like, "Curvy parts, I love you and thank you for making me whole and living this long life with me; thank you."
3. If you use lotions or oils on your body after you shower or bathe—do the same thing in the same way, saying something like, "Thank you, leg, for carrying me through this amazing journey of life where I get to experience movement."
4. Do this for a minimum of thirty days and use the following prompts in your journal.

- What part of me was I surprised to touch and why?
- What part of me did I feel the most ease touching and why?
- What part of me did I feel discomfort touching and why?

Mirror Ritual

Stand in front of a mirror and look at yourself, even for just a second if it makes you uncomfortable. Do this every day and look at yourself, bringing your eyes to your eyes. Speak to yourself with words of comfort and acceptance.

This practice gets easier the more you do it. You may feel most comfortable starting with your clothes on and then taking an item off the more you do it. Make it a ritual to see yourself.

1. Light candles and set the stage of loving awareness.
2. Set an intention (written or spoken) to connect to your body, where your spirit resides.
3. Sit or stand in front of the mirror and gaze.
4. Close your eyes for a moment after you gaze at each part of your body and feel the heat of your own gaze in that exact spot. Move back and forth, looking then feeling.
5. Use soothing or meditating sounds.
6. Anoint yourself with your favorite oils or lotions after each session to celebrate another step of connecting to your body.

Your Body and Intuition (Your Body as the Pendulum)

Connecting our body to the energy of the Earth and letting it guide us in finding the answers we seek is one of the most powerful rituals we can do. After you've done this ritual for a number of months or years, you'll no longer need the actual ritual to determine if your body is a yes or no. You'll need only to take a few breaths and you'll know.

1. To start learning how to use your body as a yes/no, you first need to learn what a "yes" and what a "no" feel like. Set time aside for seven days to ask yourself yes-or-no questions you already know the answer to. Make sure these are not ambiguous questions or the type you might feel differently about on any given day. Good subjects are your name, age, location, job, etc., anything that is static over a period of time.
2. Ask the question in a yes-or-no form out loud, then take a breath.
3. Once you feel the flow of that answer, say out loud, "This is what a yes (or a no) feels like in my body."
4. Do this for ten to twelve minutes, repeating what a yes and a no feel like.
5. I do this with one hand on my heart and one on my belly, and I ask the question with my eyes closed to tune everything out so I can *feel* the answer.
6. After seven days, try one question a day you do *not* know the answer to and repeat the process. It's best to start with questions you'll be able to determine the answer to within a couple of weeks. Good questions are about an event coming up, your (or someone else's) travel plans, a work project, house project—anything that is temporary and will resolve. Ask the question. You'll immediately feel a yes or a no—trust the first answer you feel before your mind kicks in and overanalyzes.
7. Write down the answer and move on with your day. Come back and track your daily practice often. It's OK if you get a few wrong answers at the start. Keep going.

Body Alphabet

This is a powerful tool to use when you know you aren't fully connected to your body and you want to change the disconnection and open up to deeper layers of wisdom. This ritual is simple.

1. In your journal or on any piece of paper, write out the alphabet on the left-hand side of the paper.
2. For each letter, write a part of your body and how you feel about it or a way that part is connected to nature. The goal is to use each letter as a prompt to dive into your body part by part. If you cannot find a body part that starts with that letter, use that letter as a symbol and find that item in nature and write out how your body is like that part of nature. For example, X can be a part of your body where muscles intersect.
3. Let's consider the letter A: Adam's apple, abdomen, Achilles' heel, artery, abductor, etc. A simple internet search will give you a whole list. Choose one and write it out like this:

* *My Adam's apple is a part of my throat chakra, and I feel my throat chakra is ...*
* *I hold hidden wisdom in my abdomen, and it is telling me ...*
* *The abductor is what creates stability in my hips, and my hips feel ...*
* *I connect to nature through my Achilles tendon by ...*

This is a way to connect parts of your body to feelings and track them with your writing. Once you know what you feel, you can begin working magic to support your body, which holds your soul. You can find blocked wisdom, misaligned energy, and parts that need healing and connection. Touch these parts of your body while you write about them. Go slowly through the alphabet. Take your time and really connect with each part of your body while doing this work.

Chapter Twenty
Winter Rituals

OUR BODY GOES THROUGH SEASONS, although they are not always the same as the changes we see outside. When we study the North and how it resonates at our soul level, we look at the properties of winter and can determine if our body is in a winter phase. The soul has seasons, including dark nights, explosive radiance, stormy and destructive days, and new beginnings. These are similar to how Mother Nature marks her seasons.

Seasons of the soul are powerful ways to work your growth and magic. Once you can identify what season you are in, you can feed your soul with what it needs in that season, and you can also count on the fact that the season will change. Progress, education, regression, and restart. The seasons of your soul are all connected and all are sacred.

Sacred Magic

The winter of the North brings rest and reflection to replenish our soil and tend to our roots. The East (spring) is where we go when we need to redefine our beliefs and plant new seeds of ideas or intentions. The South (summer) is where we put our intentions into action and fuel the fire behind them, and the West (autumn) is where we go to water the growth. The following are rituals to do while you are in the North. Start with the Digital Detox Ritual. This is imperative for you to begin when you are in the North. It will settle the overstimulation and improve your capacity for rest and recharging.

Wheel of Intention Ritual

1. Draw a large circle, about the size of a dinner plate, on a blank piece of paper.
2. Draw an X in the center of the circle so you have four quadrants to write in. Write your name in the center of the circle.
3. Moving sunwise, in the top quadrant, write the answer to this question: How can I show more love and devotion to my body?
4. In the right quadrant, write the answer to this question: How can I adjust my schedule to make more time for rest?
5. In the bottom portion, write the answer to this question: How do I show I love myself and how I've grown?
6. In the left section, write the answer to this question: Where do I feel the deepest connection to my gifts (list the parts of your body)?

Each part you complete on this wheel is a reflection of where you are at in the North. You can do this monthly when creating goals or plans to ensure you remain connected to your body while striving toward your goals or intentions. If you work with tarot or oracle cards, you can also draw a card before you complete each section of the wheel.

Winter Wishes Ritual

Connect to this inward time of winter and explore what you have learned about yourself and make wishes for what you want more of—sacred magic, joy, passion, and fulfillment in your life. Remember that this is merely a stop along the way, and the cycles will continue and you will be moving into the East of this day, week, month or year of your life. Making the transition between the facets of your path and life is a magical practice that says, "Yes, I'm here, but I cannot stay."

For supplies, you'll need: one white candle, several small pieces of paper, a heat-safe bowl, several dried bay leaves, a lighter or matches, and your journal.

1. Spend time with your imagination and let come forth what you want to see happen in your future.
2. Light your candle and hold the flame in your gaze as you picture it melting away any icebergs of barriers that will impact your wishes.
3. Once the list feels complete, sit with it, then one at a time, write each wish on one of the blank pieces of paper and set it aside. If any fears or worries of how that wish will happen come up, write those on a bay leaf and burn it, saying, "With this flame, I melt any barriers to this wish."
4. Drop any unburned parts into the heat-safe bowl and hold a lighter or a match to them until they are completely ash.
5. Continue until all your wishes are written on the small pieces of paper and the barriers are burned away. Discard the ashes anywhere in nature.
6. Take all the small pieces of paper and add them to an altar or any sacred space.

A powerful way to work with these wishes is to put them in a special bowl to visit often and keep adding to them throughout the year. When you next

Sacred Magic

decide to do a yearly look-ahead exercise (such as creating a vision board, goal setting, or other yearly rituals), take them out and remind yourself why you had these wishes in the first place.

Winter Crossroads Ritual

When you find yourself in the North and feeling deeply inward, it can seem like there is a physical barrier between you and the rest of the world. It is normal to feel this way when walking the North path. Yet a time will come when you will emerge from the winter, just as trees and plants do. Whether you are spending time in the North by choice or have been thrust here by life events—this ritual is good for honoring a crossroads you might find yourself at.

For supplies, you'll need: string, ribbon, or anything you can use to mark space if you are doing the ritual indoors. If you are doing it outdoors, find a natural line, preferably a liminal one, you can return to several times. It can be pavement to grass, grass to forest, any waterline, or even just the line between a building and nature. It helps if it is near your home so you can easily return to it. If it's not on your property and you are using a natural crossroads in a city, that's perfect; just make sure it's someplace you can sit. You'll also need a few fresh flowers (grown or purchased), your journal, and a bottle of water (and a bowl if you'll be indoors).

1. Find your crossroads place outdoors and track the liminal space. If you are indoors, pull a string or ribbon across your floor to mark a crossroads.
2. Sit on one side of the crossroads and speak to yourself, or aloud if possible, "This is where I am now. I know I will cross into a new time and place, but for today I am allowing myself to be here."
3. Write out what it feels like to be on this side of the crossroads and what you've learned about your own magic. Offer gratitude for how deeply

you are learning to connect to your body and to nature's wisdom, then surrender to not knowing when you'll cross into the new version of you.
4. Use the flowers to mark the crossroads by laying them out in a line or use petals of the flower. If outdoors, you can leave the flowers there. If indoors, leave them for the entirety of the ritual.
5. Pour water on the outdoor space to give the Earth a drink and say thanks. If indoors, pour some of the water into a bowl to represent giving Earth a drink.
6. Remove the crossroads if indoors and put the items aside to return to when you're ready to cross into the new version of you. If outside, leave the offerings and return when ready.
7. Allow time to go by when you are in this phase. It can be weeks or months until you are ready to move into the next phase. When you are ready, re-create or return to the same crossroads and conduct all the same steps, starting with picturing yourself when you sat there last and standing in that same place. When ready, cross over the crossroads and sit on the other side and face the center you just crossed over.
8. Journal on what part of you is being left in that place and time and how you are ready to move forward and why.

Additional layers: If I'm doing this outdoors, I also provide an offering to the spirits of the lands. Sometimes I sit in the crossroads a few times a day, sometimes daily for a month. If you can leave your space set up (inside or out) and it won't be disturbed, that's wonderful; leave it be. But either way is fine.

Chapter Twenty-One
Dreamtime Rituals

Our time while sleeping is a deeply vulnerable time that can open portals. I have experienced this regularly over the last ten years and have helped clients understand their intentions in dreamtime by opening portals. It also can be a time to shut down any spiritual or portal work and just sleep. You can choose what you want your dreamtime to be when you are clear on your intentions.

It is imperative to note that rest is the priority while sleeping. As much as I love traveling to new dimensions while I sleep, I do not intentionally do so unless I am well-rested and have the spaciousness to move slowly the morning after. I recommend you make sleep the first goal, and if the time is right, then

SACRED MAGIC

use dreamtime for traveling into the other worlds.

Often when we are not intentionally traveling the astral planes during sleep, we will receive potent messages from spirit, from our subconscious, and from the unseen worlds. We all have those nights when we wake up with a wow moment, even when we didn't plan to have that experience. Remember that choosing the sacred magic way of life is to always use intentions to choose what you want to experience. You have that same choice when it comes to dreamtime when you use evening rituals and intentions.

When creating a sacred space to support your dreamtime, make sure you keep a journal near your bed, so the moment your eyes open you can jot down anything you recall from your dreams. You should do this before you get up while you are still in the sleepy state. Dreams fade fast the moment you begin to move your body.

DREAM AND SLEEP RITUALS

If you wish to experience more vivid dreams or want to receive messages in your sleep, create an evening ritual that will support these. These steps also cover an intention for restful sleeping.

1. Use breathwork plus intentions before you go to bed. Sink into your practices and set an intention that is clear and concise.
2. Eliminate any external noise (and phones) at least thirty minutes before bed. Here is another good time to be practicing your Digital Detox Ritual.
3. I recommend writing out your intention and placing it under your pillow. Often I will include small items from my altar that represent my intentions for that night.
4. If you are working with any special plant allies or spirit guides, call them in prior to sleep to support your intention.

5. If you want to have deep rest and no vividness so you can reset and sleep, ask for that too. This is part of being in the North, knowing when it's time for rest with no magical happenings taking place. If I've had a heavy day and my body is tired and I just want to sleep, I bring a rosebud or flower to bed with me and ask it to show me the beauty, even if my energy feels heavy. This ritual is simple and works every time. Your mind and spirit are always processing during sleep, but creating intentions and rituals to focus on rest will have a huge impact on the health of your body.

I have often observed when working with students and clients and their dreamtime rituals that fear arises when spirits come during sleep, and they feel they need protection. I have several ways to look at this, and you should consider them before you embark on opening the unseen worlds during sleep.

You are in control. That is the protection you should always keep in mind. Use your voice. You can say yes or no, aloud before you sleep, to any visitors. You can aid your no with protection stones, such as black tourmaline, and place them around your bed. You can burn protective incense and create a locked-down energetic space for sleep. Just set the intention; it's not hard. But understand when you do this, you are blocking all communication. It is my belief that the fear we have about pesky spirits or invasive visits in dreams is a reflection of the fears we carry in our human experience.

Before embarking on protection, I suggest exploring your beliefs about spirits. Once you have realigned the beliefs and remember you are always in control, protection becomes much less necessary. If you perceive negative or "bad" energies in your dreams, I suggest you start looking at what you fear in your life and where this started for you. Where in your body are you carrying that energy? What heavy vibes do you take with you to bed?

As we begin looking at all the possible rituals to complete the quest for real, tangible sacred magic, we have to start by looking at what we need to remove that isn't sacred and isn't magical. Start with the Digital Detox Ritual and ensure your phone is off at least thirty minutes before sleep.

Sweet Dreams Sachet Ritual

1. As described above, set your intention before bedtime, write it down, and tuck it under your pillow.
2. Add plant allies or flowers to aid your sleep time. You can add these to a small sachet and place it under your pillow or hang it above your bed. I also suggest adding a small bowl of water under or near your bed to absorb anything not in alignment with your dream intentions. Optional: Add stones or mementos that represent your intentions (pictures, drawings, symbols, etc.).
3. Keep a journal near your bed and before your feet touch the floor in the morning, write down everything you remember before the memory of the dream starts to fade.

Dream-Activation Ritual

This is a powerful ritual and should be used only when you are ready for your psychic gifts to be more deeply awakened while you are sleeping. The impact of this ritual will not necessarily take place during sleep but will manifest itself during your waking hours. You are priming your body to receive more information while sleeping, but the information will come while you are awake. If you haven't worked your chakra system yet or aren't aware of what that is (I cover this in the second book in the series), don't worry about my reference to your third eye and just focus on the part of your face I'm describing.

The only item you'll need is your favorite crystal or any stone.

1. Start with deep belly breaths, breathing in for ten counts then out for twelve counts. This should be done while sitting on the side of your bed with your feet flat on the floor. Breathe deeply for several minutes (ten minutes is ideal).
2. Then begin breathing as if you are pulling energy through your eyes and forehead (your third eye that sits just above the place between your eyes), picturing the inhale as a blanket of energy touching your face then blowing it out in a puff. Do two rounds of this.
3. After you have the feeling down of breathing into your third eye, bring in your stone and do the inhale portion, holding your breath for a few seconds while rubbing the stone on your third eye. Then remove the stone and exhale. Do this several times until your third eye becomes warm.
4. Place the stone under your pillow while you sleep.
5. This is best done for at least thirteen nights in a row. Then return the stone to an altar for use at another time.
6. You should already have the grounding exercises and a daily journaling practice nailed down before you start this, as they both will support you in the weeks ahead.

Dreamtime Intentions

Virtually any intention, question, or desire you have can be cast prior to sleep. You can write it, speak it, wear it, or hold it in your mind's eye before sleeping. Answers will come during your dreams when you set the intention carefully and with thought.

- Do you want more vivid dreams about magic and miracles? No problem; hold that intention as you drift off.
- Do you want to awaken your body's wisdom? Hold that intention and connect to your body before you drift off.

- Do you want to remember your dreams? Hold that intention, write it out, and keep a journal close by.

Anything is possible when you make dreamtime a portal for your own growth. At the very least, dreamtime in the North should be focused on the intention of deep rest and connecting to your body.

Chapter Twenty-Two
Developing Psychic Gifts

YES, YOU HAVE PSYCHIC GIFTS and they will change and grow as you change and grow. The deeper you sink into the connection between nature and your body, the stronger your body will feel. Your psychic gifts will expand as you learn to connect to plants, sacred spaces, and dreamtime. You'll see, feel, and know that everything around you and inside you is connected. You'll feel it deeply in your human physical senses then notice your extra senses are also beginning to awaken.

Use the journey listed in the Journeying section in Part One to start reflecting on what was most present in your field when you did the journey. Could you see the landscape clearly? What did you hear, feel, smell? Was it clear or foggy? Most people will have one area of the journey that was easier to intuit. Let that guide you about which gift to start with. When you start with one sense and allow it to grow and develop, the rest will also increase. One at a time is the most powerful way.

Remember, it all comes through your body. If you want more of your psychic gifts awakened, continue the Body Rituals. Remember that your body is the conduit, so connect deeper to your body, spend time in stillness, and these gifts will naturally begin to awaken.

Light-Clearing Ritual

Start with a baseline practice every day or several times a week. You can do this before any other ritual, after a ritual, while out of balance, or anytime you want to find your center or connect deeply with it.

1. Start in a seated position with your back straight, feet flat on the floor.
2. Take several deep belly breaths and close your eyes.
3. Picture a bright light coming down from the sky and entering through the top of your head.
4. Let this bright light travel slowly down your body through every part, filling your entire body with bright white light.
5. When it reaches your feet, picture it leaving through your feet and traveling into the center of the Earth.
6. Hold the light in your mind's eye that is coming from above, moving through you, and continuing deep down.
7. Take a few more deep breaths and let this light now come up from the center of the Earth, back through your body, and up to the sky.
8. Let the light move from above you, through you, down to the Earth, and back again.

9. Hold yourself in the center of this bright, moving light as long as possible.
10. When it feels complete, let the light slow down and open your eyes.

Daily Energy Clearing

Daily work to balance your energy is important when working on your psychic gifts. It helps clear your lens and removes any unwanted energy. By now you have several rituals you should be using such as grounding, breathing, resting, connecting to your space, journaling, and most important, connecting to your body. Twice daily, choose a grounding practice or the above light-clearing practice to ensure you move and balance the energy you've either awakened with or picked up through the day.

Begin Awakening Psychic Gifts

You are the magic and setting an intention to awaken your psychic gifts is a powerful way to put your energy toward this goal. Although all the rituals in this book will activate your senses, this is a specific way to choose what to focus on first.

For supplies, you'll need: a few small pieces of paper, a pen, and a special glass, bowl, or chalice. Put these items next to your bed.

1. Start by thinking about what came to mind for you when reading about the different types of gifts in the chapter on Psychic Gifts in Part One. Choose one to start with, such as clear seeing, clear knowing, clear feeling, or any combination that feels right.
2. Using one of the small pieces of paper, write down an intention of exactly what you want to focus on—clear seeing, improved visualization, stronger inner knowing in your belly, hearing messages from

spirits, strong feeling of others' emotions, or whatever feels like a good place to start. Place it in your special container.
3. Spend ten minutes a day alerting your body to pay attention to this sense. Breathe and speak your intention out loud. Do this daily for at least thirty days to start (many of us who use this practice keep it in our weekly or monthly rituals).
4. Write down any messages this specific gift brings in throughout the day and add it to your container at night before sleep.

Continue Awakening Psychic Gifts

Creating an intention to open your psychic gifts and experience them deeply begins with connecting to your body and setting goals on practices and experiences. Like a muscle, your gifts develop at the pace you practice opening them. We'll start with an altar to support the goal of awakening your gifts, a key facet to experiencing real magic. Each one of the rituals listed below can be done on their own, or you can do a combination of them, knowing the more time and effort you put into these intentions, the faster you will begin to see your gifts coming into your field. Think of it like either taking a single sip of water or draining an entire glassful. You get to choose how quickly you awaken your gifts.

1. Write the following words on a piece of paper and place it where you can see it on an altar: *I am open to receive more magic and more connection to the unseen worlds. I receive, I receive, I receive.* Speak these words aloud and often throughout your day.
2. Determine what psychic gift you are developing as a priority at this time and add an item to each altar to represent it. I always recommend a picture of your third eye (either drawn or find one online). The third eye can also be displayed in any shape on your altar. You

may even draw it on a leaf or put your items in the shape of an eye as a symbolic reminder.

Whatever way you build your altar and whatever you feel called to create in your sacred spaces are just for you. They are an extension of you and should reflect your own personal creative power.

Chapter Twenty-Three
Additional Journeys

Working in journey space is learning how to take basic meditation and letting it open the door to other realms of possibilities. It's a combination of deep breaths, relaxing the mind, and going to the spiritual places we cannot access while living the mundane part of our lives. Journeys can be long and intricate or short bursts of trancelike states, both leading you to see the unseen and feel the unfelt thoughts, and bring them back into your human experience.

Of course, by now you are practicing regular digital detoxing and know that eliminating external noise is critical to hearing and experiencing inner wisdom. The same requirement of eliminating external noise, distractions, or influences is also required when going into journey space.

There is no right or wrong way to journey; there's only doing it or not. Our busy lives and overstimulated minds can take time to step out of the mundane and into the spiritual realms. If you want to experience more of the realms that journeys take you to, keep practicing. Spend a few minutes a day stilling your breath, closing your eyes, and letting your mind wander. Spend an hour each week taking yourself on your own journey or find a guided one to lead you.

Use the rituals below to set up your space for the longer journeys. Once you get used to going into journey space (meditation plus trance), you can begin to enter this state outside of the space you created. Start with all the necessary tools until you are acclimated to it, then attempt to do it on the fly or in between other parts of your day. The more you practice, the easier it will be.

Setting Up Space for Journeys

Whether you're doing this work in meditation or through breathwork, creating a space for journeys is about creating a sanctuary that provides the energy of surrender.

This may include finding a location that removes unwanted distractions and making it comfortable with pillows, soft blankets, or a chair for sitting up if you prefer. Your space for journeys may be the same space where you do other activities and where you keep a stack of comfort items nearby, so if you want to journey, you have the items handy.

What I teach students is you can journey, meditate, or do any rituals in any place—outside sitting in nature, waiting to pick up your child from school, or, like me, while waiting at the doctor's office. It's a matter of stilling your mind and allowing the surrender to occur.

You are the magic. It's in you and through you. You might wonder what the specific tools for awakening your psychic gifts are, and my answer is that

Additional Journeys

they are crafted purposefully into each one of the rituals in this book. Use them and you'll see.

Journey to the Beach of Time

After the A Journey for You script in Part One, the fifth contemplation question is about a place in the past or in the future you might want to visit. Here is a way to set up the journey to go where you choose.

1. All journeys start with setting up a comfortable space, turning off all distractions, and having a journal nearby for recording afterward. I suggest at least thirty minutes to complete this journey.
2. Spend three to five minutes meditating or deep belly breathing, preferably lying down with your eyes closed.
3. Start by picturing yourself on a beach, alone on the beach with beautiful sand and the ocean in front of you. Slowly walk your way to the ocean. You're going to get into the water and swim to the left if you want to visit a time in the past, or you'll swim to the right if you are visiting a time in the future.
4. Focus: Walk into the water slowly, swim in the calm waters, then move to the right or the left. In the journey you will float. While you are floating, go to that place in time you want to visit. Let your body feel light and move gently with the ocean and visit the place in your mind.
5. If you have questions for that time, ask them. You'll be able to be in the ocean in the journey and experience the time you wish.
6. Keep floating and holding the timeline you are visiting.
7. When you are done, swim back the way you came and return to the beach. It may take you several tries to get the answers you want from the journey to the past or future. Sometimes we aren't meant to know all the details, so focus on why you want to visit that time.

8. Take a few moments to stretch your body, then clap your hands a few times to ensure you return to the present moment.
9. Pay attention in the days after the journey; you will often get insights in your waking world about what you asked, as all the relevant information doesn't necessarily arrive during the journey itself.
10. Write it all down. I cannot stress this enough. When you work from altered states, you are not going to remember what occurred; you must write it down to bring it to the forefront of your memory.

Journey to Meet Your Ancestors

You can use this ritual to connect with land spirits or ancestors (or spirit guides, although I will cover that more in the second book, on the East).

1. All journeys start with setting up a comfortable space, turning off all distractions, and having a journal nearby for recording afterward. I suggest at least thirty minutes to complete this journey.
2. Spend three to five minutes meditating or deep belly breathing, preferably lying down with your eyes closed.
3. This is a journey you will lead on your own; when you are breathing and relaxing, focus on your intention to meet your spirit guides. Speak the intention aloud on the exhale. It can be, "I am relaxing deeper and deeper to prepare to meet you" or "I call my spirit guides forth to meet me in this journey." Then in your mind's eye, take yourself to a forest and walk around. Let your visualization abilities kick in. See the trees, feel them, and connect to nature as an entry point on this journey.
4. While you are wandering, allow a faint light to appear ahead of you and slowly make your way toward the light.

Additional Journeys

5. You'll see the light is a large bonfire with logs for sitting down around the fire. When you are close, sit by the fire and wait for your guides to arrive.
6. Remain there and let them interact with you. Sometimes you'll see them, sometimes you'll hear them, and sometimes neither will happen. Keep waiting. This journey takes practice for you to be able to be very calm and connected to nature (which creates the frequency for your guides to come). You cannot do it wrong. If they do not come, try again another day and pay attention to any messages that come in the meantime.
7. When you've stayed as long as you can or when your mind starts to wander, step away from the fire, go back to the forest, and calibrate to nature before coming back out.
8. Take a few moments to stretch your body, then clap your hands a few times to ensure you return to the present moment.
9. Write down everything—it all matters.

Part Three
The Wheel Turns

Chapter Twenty-Four
The Final Ritual of the North

Magic is already happening inside you every moment of the day. Life becomes sacred when we seek to understand the meaning of our own lives. When we study magic, we are studying the meaning behind transformation. The path reveals itself when we choose to see it through the lens of the elements in each direction. We have found ourselves here on this path and have zoomed out to see the whole of our lives as one giant interconnected map of experiences and feelings. All these experiences are happening inside our body, but only for a limited time. We have an expiration date; the clock is ticking with every day that goes by.

For our final ritual in the North we are going to further anchor into why we are here and what purpose our soul wants to live. The most powerful way to do this is to contemplate what you want to be remembered for. When we contemplate what we want to be remembered for, we are exploring what will really matter to our spirit when it has left our body.

What we keep hidden are truths we refuse to look at and heal, and we are blocking the entire magic of the universe and not really living at all. If we want to live, truly live, we need to never forget that we will die—at least our physical body in this lifetime will.

For this reason, the final ritual is to write your own obituary to define how you want to be remembered.

Write Your Own Obituary

This ritual's goal is to bring in the big perspective of your life and for you to see what matters to you most. When you are on your deathbed and have taken time to consider what really matters to you and realize you have lived it, your time to transition to another place will be without regret. That's the goal of living in sacred magic, learning to live life to its fullest. You may wish to do this once a year to see the changes and desires this quest has awakened.

1. Start by setting aside time to do this powerful work without distraction.
2. Light a candle and focus on deep breathing.
3. Imagine if you were to find out you had only a few months left to live (which is actually possible since we never know when our time is up—even the greatest psychics cannot predict this).
4. Journal on these questions first: How do I want to be remembered? What would the people I love remember and say about me?
5. Then write your own obituary.

6. Once you've written it and defined how you want to be remembered, ask, "Am I living to my own full potential? If not, why not?"
7. Start a new page in your journal and write out what changes you can make to begin living more aligned with what truly matters to you.
8. Finish the ritual with a strong "I AM" statement that defines how you are going to embrace the alignment you seek. For example, "I AM connecting more deeply with my body and moving more freely in it."
9. To end the ritual, play your favorite song as loud as you can (either through speakers or headphones) and move your body and dance while repeating your I AM statement over and over. This will help anchor the statement into your body.

Chapter Twenty-Five
The Wheel Turns

The stop we've made here in the North is just the beginning. Time will move, our body will age, and our thoughts and beliefs will change as we grow. The North provides the quiet, cocoon-like energy to go inward and explore the foundation of who we are and who we are not.

Yet we cannot stay in the North. After we've been here for a day, a week, a month, or a year, we will change and move to the East where the seeds we've planted in the North will begin to take root.

The North has been our first stop on the quest to finding what we deem as sacred and discovering magic along the way. Our body and its connection to nature is the foundation of living openly in our own magical way.

We can call upon the spirit of the North as part of the cycle we live each day by detoxing from our addiction to social media and putting our feet on the Earth.

We can call upon the spirit of the North as part of the cycle we live in each week when we tend to the devotion of our homes and altars.

We can call upon the spirit of the North as part of each moon cycle when we allow our body time to rest and our manifestations to come forth from that rested place.

We can call upon the spirits of the North as part of the cycle we live each year in recognizing each time we've returned to the North and using its support of our quest to surrender into what we know about ourselves and our soul, and how we define heaven on Earth.

Connection to the power of the North is always present; even when we don't recognize it, it's there. There are cycles within each cycle, and we are a living embodiment of these cycles in our lives and the emotions we feel. Taking each moment out, one at a time—each memory, lesson, and nugget of wisdom and desire—and knowing what it feels like puts us in direct flow with the rhythm of the universe.

Wherever you began this journey with me and wherever you are now, it's all connected and it's all sacred. Take a moment to look inward and hold the connection with who you were, who you are, and who you will become as the holiest of all things holy. We are in a continual dance with change. This time in the North has been a series of explorations, seeking a slice of magical connection and deep levels of truth. We've only just begun this journey, allowing it to unfold one magical layer at a time.

If your heart craves more peace and joy, it starts by delving into the deepest parts of your own roots, as you've done here. If your body craves expansive, magical wonders, it starts by seeing the magic in nature, for nature is a reflection of you. If you have career or financial goals, it starts by knowing yourself and clearing your energy, allowing you to create intentionally from a place of alignment. Growth comes from knowing yourself and where you desire to change and how you desire to feel as you change.

At the beginning of this book, I shared that the more I learn, the more I change, and I know you do too. If you've only been reading this book and have yet to put any of it into motion in your life, ask yourself why. Is it because of a busy schedule? Or is there a small, lingering fear of what lies deep within your own body that still needs to be cleared? Be honest with yourself. There are many paths to awaken the magic and freedom we all deeply desire to connect to, because we know this freedom is what will guide us to our reason for incarnating here in the first place.

However, any path that promises it will be as easy as reading this book is not the full truth. Accessing deep levels of sacred magic can happen only when we go through periods of allowing ourselves to be undefined so we can experience something new. If we do only what we've always done, we will always have the same outcome. If you want a new outcome in your life, one that is filled with magic and wonder regardless of how difficult or challenging your life has been or may become again, you have to do life differently. There is no other way to experience complete transformation without opening yourself to see and experience life differently.

When we change and begin to experience life differently, then cast our new intentions out into the world, real magic happens. Real magic is what witches do when they know how to create change in their lives and the lives of others. It isn't a simple manifestation spell or boiling chicken bones in a cauldron; it's connecting to all things and finding the connection in your body. It's creating lifelong change and developing a path to live your soul's great purpose. That's witch work. Creating an enchantable life is the purpose of sacred magic and anyone can do it.

Discovering yourself is deep work; it's the Great Work of your entire lifetime. Any effort you put into studying and developing the best version of yourself is worth it, but it doesn't mean it will always be easy. Plants and the natural world will ease the journey for your body. Spirits and ancestors will aid you in this quest. Your body will begin to reveal its unique, potent form of inner knowing to a level you didn't realize was possible. You can clear old, stagnant ways of being, directly impacting your prosperity, relationships, friendships, and family. When you change, everything changes. It's as simple as that.

Thank you for allowing me to walk along with you on this journey. With each word I wrote, I could see you reading it, and I felt our connection, between us and between nature, melding into one gigantic beautiful forest of trees. My tree roots will share water with yours when yours become dry. Your branches will provide shelter for others who are learning to grow as a tree grows.

It's all sacred and it's all connected.

Chapter Twenty-Six
Resources

Author's Note

To study the real magic that exists in our lives and on this planet is to study transformation. It has been my pleasure to walk this way of life with you. First and foremost, I am a student of life, changing and growing alongside you each day. As a teacher of the mysteries, I hold this work sacred, with teaching as my method of creating transformation for myself and for those called to study real magic. Thank you for choosing me as your guide. I will continue to hold the highest vision of you possible close to my heart.

Sacred Magic

Bonus resources can be found at Tahverlee.com/northresources.

All books, including the *Sacred Magic Journal* and *Sacred Magic Oracle Deck,* can be found by visiting www.tahverlee.com.

Connect with Tahverlee on the following platforms:

- tahverlee.com

- Instagram: @tahverlee

- TikTok: @athena_in_my_blood

- Moon Temple Mystery School: moontempleschool.com

- YouTube: @Tahverlee

- Spotify (for all my playlists): @athena_in_my_blood

- You can find the Moon Temple Mystery School podcast on any of your favorite listening platforms.

Made in the USA
Middletown, DE
16 March 2025